There isn't a person alive who won't be touched by death. A universal experience, we must all face it sooner or later—in a parent, a grandparent, a child, a dear friend. Although the experience can come close to home, so few of us are prepared when it happens, prepared to deal with the emotions death stirs up, prepared to deal with our surprising reactions to something we always knew would occur but never really expected.

A comforting guide to help you through that first difficult week, then month, then year, this thoughtful handbook helps you handle the problems, the fears, the guilt, the unhappiness, and eventually, the letting go, simply, thoughtfully, and compassionately.

THE THOUGHT-A-WEEK GUIDES: HOW TO COPE WITH GRIEF

A Blue Cliff Editions Book

Judith Sara Schmidt

BALLANTINE BOOKS • NEW YORK

Library of Congress Catalog Card Number: 88-92822

ISBN 0-345-35789-2

Printed in Canada

First Edition: June 1989

To Leslie
and to Madame Collette Aboulker Muscat,
who opened the blue gate
to imagination and havanah for me

CONTENTS

Acknowledgments   xi
Introduction   1

1. I begin to grieve when I learn that someone
   close to me is terminally ill.   5
2. Writing can bring comfort.   9
3. What does it mean to me to lose this person?   13
4. I let the dying know they can leave me and
   be at rest.   17
5. I let my love be known.   21
6. I forgive, and I accept forgiveness.   25
7. My heart guides me to make final decisions.   30
8. I complete unfinished business.   34
9. I help the child within me to say good-bye.   38
10. I may want to express something personal
    at the memorial or funeral service.   42
11. I help the child within me to attend the
    service and funeral.   45
12. Rituals can help me.   48
13. Death teaches me about letting go.   51

14. I take the time to be with my loss. 55
15. I deal with the belongings that are left. 59
16. I may feel numbness as part of my grief. 63
17. I welcome the consolation of family and friends. 66
18. I live through the long nights. 71
19. Guilt and remorse may be part of my grief. 75
20. Anger is a natural grief feeling. 78
21. Sometimes I feel like a lost child. 82
22. I let the pain move through me. 85
23. Sometimes I feel depressed and need to move through my grief physically. 89
24. The only way through grief is to face it. 92
25. Little things may trigger my grief unexpectedly. 96
26. In grieving, it is also myself that I mourn for. 98
27. Through grief I discover tenderness. 101
28. My dreams can show me the way. 104
29. I choose my personal ritual of remembrance. 107
30. Life calls to me tenderly. 111
31. Death cannot shatter love. 114
32. What do life and death mean to me? 116
33. Out of this darkness, my creativity can be born. 121
34. I learn to hear the voice of aloneness. 125
35. The mysteries of birth and death are entwined. 128
36. I look at life with a new amazement. 132
37. The voice of my loneliness can guide me. 134
38. I sing a song even when it is a sad song. 137
39. New loved ones gradually enter my life. 141
40. Knowing grief, I can help others in their time of loss. 144
41. The spirit of my loved one is alive. 147
42. Sometimes grief feels as though it will go on forever. 149

43. I live open to the unknown.   152
44. I learn to live with acceptance.   155
45. Life becomes simpler for me.   157
46. The human family becomes my family.   159
47. The planet becomes my concern.   161
48. I live in the awareness of my own death.   164
49. I try to understand all of this.   166
50. Life goes on. . . . Death goes on.   168
51. Where am I?   172
52. A prayer for going on.   175

ACKNOWLEDGMENTS

I want to thank my friends and patients, who have taught me through sharing their griefs; Jason Shulman, for inviting me to write this book; and Toni Rachiele, for her fine editing.

"This book is like a wonderful, sensitive friend . . . just the right companion at a time of loss."
Ram Dass

Introduction

Birth and death are what we can be sure we all have in common. That is why I can write this introduction and this book, talking to you personally, knowing that in birth and death we are not alone, that you know me and I know you.

I am reminded of an old tale of a mother whose child is ill and dying. She goes to the wise old leader of her village to ask him to save her child. He tells her, "Your child shall be saved when you find a tiny mustard seed in a house in this village where no one has died." And so the forlorn mother begins to travel from house to house, knocking at each door and asking, "Please, if no one has died in this house, give me a mustard seed that my little one may be healed." Of course, at each house she hears only "But here a father has died," "Here our mother," "Here a grand-mother," "Here a child." And so she returns to the old wise man and tells him that in no house could she find what she was looking for, for everywhere someone had been lost to the family. And so the old man told the tearful mother, "All that I can give you is the solace of knowing that you are not alone."

And so it is. The season of death comes to all of us. A man not yet thirty years old begins to question his mortality, for his father has just had bypass surgery and his best friend's mother has just had a stroke, and life has come to seem fragile to him. He remembers how, when he was a teenager, he used to sit by a lake at night at his grandparents' summer place and look out at the sky and wonder about life and how imponderable it was, how infinite. And then he stopped pondering. He grew up, went on to law school, and became successful. And now, once again, he is looking at the large questions of life and death that loom in front of him like that vast sky of his early years.

All of us will know—or have already come to know—the agonizing cut we feel in our physical body when someone we love dies. This cut is particularly acute if a person dies suddenly and we have not had the time to prepare ourselves for the loss. Every one of us knows or will know what grief feels like: how tears will not stop for a long time, how we feel they will never stop, how they do stop—and then return when we least expect it. Perhaps when we see a beautiful sunset, hear lovely music, feel the first spring rain, look into the eyes of a loved one. Our hearts are made to hold love and loss, and there the two are forever intermixed.

No one can chart a course for how long grief will last. For each person it is different. For each loss it is different. The course of grief has its own inner timetable. Just as no one can force the daffodils to open or the birds to sing before their time, no one can force the sorrow at losing a loved one to close its wound. Wounds must heal in their own time. And for most of us they close and open and close and open, over and over again.

There are ways, however, that we can live through sorrow, ways that we can go on with love to sanctify life.

It is my hope that the fifty-two weekly Thoughts contained in this little book will help you to find ways of solace. Each of them grows out of my own meetings with grief: the sudden death of my daughter when she was four; the loss of my dearest sister-friend at the prime of her life; the long dying of my father; the dying of my dog, who died while this book was being written.

All of these losses have taught me, each in their own way, about how to make the death of a loved one not more bearable but more meaningful. For this apparently most meaningless, most absurd of all events in life must be given meaning by those who go on living, for what is even more unbearable than death is to live without meaning. Perhaps the ways in which we find meaning are helped by what we do with our grief, what we accept of it, how we allow it to be. When my daughter died, I thought darkness would never end. I did not know how I could live on in such a totally senseless universe. I felt that life, or even God, had shot my child down like some crazy person who shoots into a crowd, killing randomly. And yet, I did go on.

The things I write about in these weekly Thoughts are some of the ways that helped me to go on. I want to share these ways with you. They have been the ways I have found from deep within my grieved heart and soul, from the ancient ways of my tradition, from loving ones showing me the paths back to living. You will find your ways within your own heart, from your own tradition, from the gifts of solace your loved ones bear to you. And perhaps what I have found may also give you solace along the way. I hope so.

In the end, after all is said and done, there is only one

thing that endures, that is indestructible. And that is the love that arises out of the well of grief. That in itself is a mystery. And yet it is the only thing I am certain of about death and dying and sorrow and loss. In the end we are left holding what we started out with: love and life. Only now it is a love and sense of life that are even more precious because we know that they do not last forever. Love turns all things. Love turns grief toward life. And so it is that out of a grief turned to love I write to you.

I begin to grieve when I learn that someone close to me is terminally ill.

Grieving is about loss. Death is a final parting from which we cannot hope for return. We begin to grieve when we know someone is going to leave us. We know because someone has told us—the doctor, or our loved one's family and friends, or our loved one. Or we know because we know, because our loved one knows and, either through words or a look or a touch, tells us that the end is near. During these last months, weeks, or days, life may look ordinary from the outside. We may sit together, talk together, eat together, walk together, laugh together. We may even believe that death will not come. Something will intervene, the doctor was wrong, it's just not so.

In the beginning, we try everything. We go to every possible doctor. We are fighting, exhausting every possibility to find the person, the treatment, the medicine that will reverse the news that we have been given that nothing can be done. Even after trying everyone, everything, we may still believe that death will not come.

This is not the same as hoping without hope, having

faith till the end that where there is life, there is hope. Hoping without hope leads to final acceptance of loss and bereavement. It is a later step on the journey of loss. In the beginning, our belief that death will not come is a denial of its very reality. Death seems too final and stark for us to take in, so the denial serves to protect us. Our loved one may be experiencing the same denial.

As the curtain of denial lifts, we may find that we have let death in but are still trying to avert it, turn it around, get rid of it. How can such a thing be possible, that we can do nothing, have no control at all over this leaving? It goes against the grain of our belief that with love we can move mountains. And eventually the realization that we cannot move death, that here we are truly helpless, may make us terribly angry—at ourselves, at our loved one, at life, at God.

We may feel we have failed. If we had done this or not done that, death would not be happening. But ask yourself, in the quietness of your solitude, What more could you have done? The likelihood is that everything that could have been done has been attempted, and more. In your heart, tell yourself, "I have done everything I could. I am truly powerless. That does not mean I do not love. I am not a bad person. I am a good husband, wife, son, daughter, mother, father, friend. I have just reached the limit of what I can do. I will let go. I will begin to grieve. I will begin to hope without hope."

You may feel that it is wrong to have feelings of grief toward someone who is alive, but there is no "wrong feeling" in the process of grief. These feelings are slowly preparing you to let go. You cannot prepare the steps of your grief as if from some recipe. You have your own emotional and spiritual rhythm to follow in dealing with your loss. Let yourself be with this rhythm in an accepting way. Feel free to talk with a friend, with your clergy person, with a bereavement counselor. These people are there to help you. You may be so engrossed in tending to the person who is dying that there is no room for you, for your feelings, for your tears. It is important to make room for yourself. Let yourself be aware of where you are along the path of grieving for the person who is soon to leave you. It helps to be aware of denial, of anger, of bargaining for life, of depression. As we stand in these feelings and go through them, we come more easily to a final acceptance that death is coming and that it is inevitable. It is all right to be just where you are.

Yesterday, I went to the newspaper store. The owner was not her cheerful self. When I asked her if everything was all right, she said that her elderly mother was in the hospital, with tubes in her for all kinds of things. She wept to see her mother like this. She hurt because her mother was in a coma and didn't even know she was there. She said that she goes every day and just sits with her mother and strokes her forehead. She would like them to remove the tubes and let her mother go, but she wishes the doctors would decide to do that, for she cannot take the responsibility.

I said to her, "You are saying good-bye to her. It takes time to say good-bye." She wept and said that she was getting ready to let her mother go. It takes time to let go of the thread that connects two people in life.

This week, buy a notebook. Get one that has no lines so that you will be able to draw in it if you wish to. It will be best if you have a notebook as you read through this book, because I will be suggesting things for you to write about.

In your notebook this week, write down whatever it is you feel about what is happening with your loved one. Write any feelings of grief you are aware of. You do not need to write much. A word, a sentence, a dream. You may want to talk to your loved one in your notebook, say things you are unable to say face-to-face. Writing these things can help you decide what is best said and best not. This notebook can become your companion through this journey of grief and help you through it. It can particularly serve you when you first hear news that there is a terminal illness. As time goes on, finding words for your feelings will help you shed light on where you are, on how to go, on how to listen and follow your heart. Take at least five minutes each day this week. Sit quietly. Know your feelings and take a moment to write them.

Writing
can bring comfort.

I began to keep a journal shortly after my daughter, Leslie, died. It was a pocket-size book that I still have, twenty years later. I carried two things with me for a long time. Sunglasses because I never knew where or when the tears would come, and my little book. I carried my book because it became like a compass for me at times when I felt lost at sea, without words or direction.

Leslie died in May. I can recall one summer day shortly after. It was drizzling, a soft summer rain. I walked through the park holding Leslie's little blue umbrella over my head. I could hear the raindrops falling on it, falling like my tears. I remember stopping under a tree, taking out my book, and knowing that my bereftness needed to speak, to find words. Today I looked in that notebook to find what I had written standing there under that tree so long ago:

I cannot bear the rain today
pouring down

While I walk under
> your little blue umbrella
> holding what I can of you

I cannot bear the sun either
> pouring warmth all over me

My arms ache to spread
> mother wings around you
> swoop you up
> hold you to my breast

My fingers cry to wipe the tears
> from your eyes

To have these little journals that I carried with me was to have myself. To find the words to unspeakable feelings is to find ourselves. The words are us. The words are our tears being spoken. Our tears being rooted into some meaning, into some sense. Tears are trying to speak, to bring us to ourselves. We can be walking somewhere, sitting somewhere, waking out of a sleep, or rising out of a sleepless bed and hear something within. This is the time to open a journal. The journal becomes our compass. We hear ourselves speak and we find ourselves. And in that moment we are anchored because we have spoken, no longer lost in an unspeakable sea of sorrow, drowning in tears or anger or numbness.

Anything can be written in a journal. It is meant for no one but yourself. It is utterly private. It becomes like a dear friend who is always there and to whom anything can be said. There are things that may still remain unsaid to someone who is gone. It can all be said in your journal, simply.

I shall always love you and miss you.
It will be so hard not to hear you on

>   the phone, not to take a walk with you,
>   not to have breakfast on Sunday mornings,
>   not to, not to, not to . . . It's like being
>   a little kid and my best friend moved away. . . .
>   Who on the block will I play with?

Simple things like missing a friend on a Sunday morning can be written. Deep things like hurt or hate can be written. With no one but yourself to know what is written in your journal, there is nothing that cannot be said. The only one to hide your words from here becomes yourself. I have found that the greatest pain in my life has come from the feelings I would not let myself feel, from the words I would not let myself hear, from the tears I would not let myself cry. All of these that I would not, could not, share with another I could ultimately share with my intimate friend, my journal.

Sometimes I look back at what I have written. Some pages have a single word written. For example, in a dark hour I wrote the word "light" with a yellow crayon and colored a yellow circle around it. When I look at that page today, I can see that it was a prayer for light to come into my darkness. I can also find quotations that I had written to either console or guide myself, things I had read somewhere that struck some deep chord in me, like the one I find now as I thumb through an old journal:

> There are parts of our hearts whose existence we do not yet know and suffering has to anchor them to make us aware of their existence.
>
> —Le Bloy

Finding our words for our suffering can help to bring that awareness to our hearts. During this week, find the

book that is best for you to write in. It can be a plain
loose-leaf or a bound notebook. It can be cloth-covered. It
can be a pretty one that catches your eye because of its
color or pattern. Take your time in the store. Let the book
call to you. It will be your companion for quite some time.
Certainly through the weekly readings in this book you will
use your notebook. As you write in your journal while
reading this book, you will be making a record of your
journey through grief and solace. It will be best to choose a
book that has unlined pages so that you can draw in it when
you wish to. When you buy your book, you can also buy a
set of colored pencils.

As you sit with your new book and colored pencils,
open to the first blank page. Open the box of pencils. Take
out the one color that you respond to most strongly. Take
this pencil, place it beside your book. Now, just sit with
your eyes closed for a while. Just breathe quietly until you
hear within you the one word that wants to be spoken. Let
yourself hear the one word that will express where you
want this journey to lead you. Let yourself listen. Now
write this word in the center of the first page and encircle it
in gold so that it holds your prayer. Each day this week, set
aside some time to write in your journal, to use your pencils if you want to.

What does it
mean to me
to lose this person?

As I write this, I am sitting at a window, overlooking a long stretch of low, rolling mountains. In this stillness, they seem to have been here forever, to roll on forever. A lone bird sings out the window. As I look past the mountains, past the curtains of morning mist that hang over them, I sense the other side, the far side of the mountains, the distance beyond, and I imagine how, there, where I cannot reach to, are those I have lost: daughter, friend, lover, father, dog. I smile, for they are so far away and yet so close to me in the light and the silence of this morning.

Each one of these beings is intricately woven into the tapestry of my life. As each one departed from my life, a thread pulled out, leaving an empty space in the tapestry. Empty spaces where there had been unique color, form, pattern, that each person had woven and entwined with my life. Empty spaces, gaping holes in the tapestry that take time to reweave, never the same and never replaceable.

What does it mean for you, now, to be losing this person in your life? To have the threads that this person has woven into your life begin to unravel? Is it a father or mother, a husband or wife, a child, a sister or brother, a friend you are losing? Wrapped up in these words are the many intimate meanings that are contained in those deep relationships that are interwoven with our lives. We don't know, really, what they mean to us until the person is gone, until the space is empty.

But it is good to know what someone means to us, even in the small ways we can know this before a person goes. If we do, we can look at a loved one and show with our eyes, with our words, what this relationship means for us, what we will miss. There is still time to show and to share mutual gratitude.

You may want to take your journal at a time when you can sit quietly and write to the person you are losing or have lost to tell them what they mean to you, what this loss means to you. If for some reason you cannot share these thoughts, it doesn't matter, for in the writing you will have opened your heart, and this openness will talk.

As you write in your journal, or are simply thinking about what it means for you to lose this person, you may find that there are negative memories or feelings that come to you. Most of us are disturbed by this, for we believe that at a time like this we should be all-loving, all-caring. But relationships are no different before, during, or after death. Relationships go on and on to be worked through. That is what relationship is for, to help us to grow, to help us to learn to love. So allow these negative feelings to be if they are there for you. Know that as you accept them, as you let them be a part of all that you are experiencing now, you are making room for your other feelings to be alive as well. If you are using your energies to push down negative feelings that you think you should not have, you are probably also pushing down the positive feelings that are within you, and if you do this, you are bound to be tight and not fully able to share this time of farewell.

In order to help yourself to experience the myriad feelings in your relationship, let yourself enter this exercise: Find a comfortable place for yourself. Sit down or lie down, and make sure your clothing is not restricting or uncomfortable. Close your eyes. Feel yourself breathing. Be still, be quiet. From within yourself, see yourself holding a ball. It is a ball made of layers that you can peel away. This is the ball of your relationship with the person you are losing, who is being released from the tapestry of your life, whose spirit is going over the mountain to another place beyond all the layers of relationship. Now see yourself peeling away one layer at a time: disappointment in what this relationship has not given you; exhaustion because this person has burdened you through illness; anger because of the burdens you are left with; guilt for your anger, or for your lacks during your relationship. Peel away these layers, one by one, honesty by honesty. And then, when it is all peeled away, see if there is one more layer to peel, one layer that is hardest for you to look at, to name. See it, name it. Peel it away. And now, see that what remains in the palm of your hand is the very heart, the essence, the core of your relationship. See what it is. A diamond, a grain of sand, a star, a pearl, a flower, a smile, a tear? And know that it can never be lost or destroyed. It is what will fill the empty spaces of your tapestry with love. For love is what you hold in your hands. Take it, place it in your heart. There it will form the threads with which to reweave your tapestry.

If you cannot find the core now at the heart of this ball, know that even so it is there, hidden until such time as all the layers hiding it are peeled away. Some of our relationships are so complicated, with so many layers from the past, that we need to accept that we may not be able to reach what is at the center, perhaps not now, perhaps not ever. This, too, is part of making peace with our losses, with giving ourselves the solace of knowing that we will go on working through this relationship until we bring it to some peace, even after the person is gone.

I let the dying know they can leave me and be at rest.

Nina was my friend for over thirty years, one of the friends I call sister-friends that I have been blessed with. Just before her fiftieth birthday, Nina began to weaken after a year-long struggle with cancer. She was bedridden at home; it became clear that she was exhausted and losing a valiant battle. But Nina would not let go. Why should she? She was young, vibrant, filled with love and talents to give to life. She never spoke of dying, and thus none of us close to her had the opportunity to let her know she could leave us. Perhaps Nina thought of leaving us, but it was unspoken—a secret, although not a well-hidden one. Why should it not have been unspeakable?

Nina had two sons, fourteen and eighteen. Jess, the younger, had had difficulty in school, and Nina had rallied her energies, allowing herself to become bedridden only after making sure that he was settled in an appropriate high school. Nina continued to have concerns about Jess, who was still living at home. In this home, life went on as usual, as if death were not going to come, as if Nina were going to recover. But before our eyes, she was not recovering. Nor could she let go. Nor could we let her know that we could let her go.

One afternoon, on my way to Nina's house, I lost the back portion of a sweater I was knitting for her. And I knew then that I had let go. When I arrived at her home, I told Nina and Jess what had happened. I could see on their faces that I was acting and speaking what everyone had silently agreed should remain unspoken.

A week later, as I arrived for my morning visit, Jess was sitting on the edge of Nina's bed. Nina had had a very bad night. She turned to me and said, "You know, last night, in the middle of the night, I called to Jess. He came and sat by my bed. He said, 'Mom, it's getting too difficult for both of us. It's okay if you die.'" Shortly after, other friends arrived. We sat around Nina's bed under the window. The birds sang the sweet sounds of life, as we all let go. Two hours later, Nina was gone.

During that night, I found myself lighting a candle. I found myself talking to Nina's spirit, for I sensed that she still needed something more to assure her that it was all right to go, finally to be at rest. I told her, "It's all right. Be at peace. Your children will be well loved, well cared for, and safe. They will have a home and all the security they need. Be at peace."

There is always a nagging doubt when we follow our heart's instinct to do something like speak to someone who has already died, but we need to trust and follow this instinct of the heart, because the heart may contain a knowing of the person who has gone that our mind might perhaps see as stupid.

People who are dying do hold on to us out of their love and devotion to us, just as we hold on to them. No loving person wishes to separate when they know they are needed.

And so it is up to us to face our need not to let this person go. Sometimes we cannot bear to let go lest we think it is some failure on our part to heal with our love. Sometimes we literally do not think we can go on without this person. Each of us must meet what it is in us that will not let go. You can do this by sitting in solitude or with a close friend or relative and, out loud, giving voice to these feelings.

A woman of seventy told me, "I won't let him go. I've been married to him for fifty years. I don't know how to live without him. I'm not ready to die and I can't live alone. He can't leave me yet." Then, deep tears softened her anxiety. Shortly after, she approached her husband's hospital bed, took his hands, and looking into his eyes, said, "Sam, you have been a good husband to me. I love you. I don't want you to suffer anymore. It's okay with me for you to go. I love you." Softly, after months of suffering, Sam held his wife's hands and let himself slip away.

Sometimes we cannot let a person hear in words that we are letting them go. Perhaps they are not able to accept the reality, or perhaps we are not yet able to speak of it. But our eyes can speak, our tender touch can speak. Sometimes a person has already gone and we are still slowly letting them go. Then we can speak to them as I spoke to my friend Nina after she had gone. There are things we may not have known about when our loved one was still alive, things we did not have words for. We can say these words whenever they enter our hearts. Perhaps we can be heard. We do not know. No matter. What matters is that we let our heart speak.

This week, let your heart speak. Hear, within yourself, what you are holding on to. See if you can loosen this hold somewhat. Perhaps not all the way. But even saying, "I will not, cannot let you go yet. Not ever," is already a loosening. Whatever loosening you have experienced, there is no doubt that the other, the one who is doing the work of letting go into death, will be grateful for your tender blessing that he may go in peace and in your love.

I let my love
be known.

For many of us it is not always easy to show our love. It is strange, but we are often too shy to reveal what is in our hearts to those to whom we are closest: parents, mates, children, best friends. How many times have you said to yourself, "Oh, I'll give her a hug tomorrow. . . . I'll reach my hand out another time"? There seems to be a reticence to open the doors of our hearts fully and to let come out, like a spontaneous child, the naked good feelings that are there.

Most of us are like this. Perhaps we do not like to experience the embarrassment that may go with revealing what is in our hearts. Or we are vulnerable and do not want to risk receiving less than a fully loving response from the other. With children, most of us can show our love freely, because children are so generous with their own love. They run toward us, embrace us, lift up faces that are open like flowers with their trusting love. Yet we withhold the expression of our love from adults.

But here you are with someone for whom the tomorrows

are numbered. You say, "I'll show my love tomorrow, next week, sometime soon. . . . I'll wait for the right moment . . . maybe on his birthday . . . maybe on our anniversary. . . . I'll think of something special to show my special feelings." And if we are honest, we will know that we are really looking for a way to cover our feelings with a gift, a treat, "something special," when the most special gem in all the world is the pure, unadorned, simple feeling of love that we hold out in our hand, in our eyes, and give unreservedly to those we cherish. When we do this, we are giving them our trust, our humility and humanity, our childlike being.

"Tomorrow" is so clearly what it always is: an illusion. For no one of us knows what tomorrow will bring, what the next moment will bring. Now, when you are close to someone so ill that they are here for precious little time, tomorrow means even less. Today, this moment, this time together is everything, is all there ever will be, is a precious gift of life.

As you read this, you may be saying to yourself, "But she is suffering so much; she is so depressed; I don't want to upset her; better to keep things superficial." Listen to these things that you say to yourself that seem like good reasons not to show your love. Your loved one may be connected to tubes, may be ravaged by illness and just not look like the person you love; he may be irritable with pain, or angry, or sunk in despair. You may feel that there is no room in this emotional atmosphere for any expression of love. You may even feel alienated by all the barriers, emotional and medical, that stand between you and your loved one.

Just as in life, so it is in the face of dying. There are myriad blocks to expressing what is within us. Within yourself, the blocks may be made of fear of the changed person you see before you, or of anger that he is going to leave you here without him, or of a need to show a mask of strength to let the dying person know you are not suffering. Whatever you are doing to block the expression of your love, know that your loved one is doing similar things, dealing with his own barriers, feeling isolated as well, because anytime we block the expression of love, we do feel isolated.

Sit quietly each day this week, knowing how much you want to overcome any isolation. Close your eyes. Look inside for the block to showing your love. See what it is. Accept that it is there. Do you feel so guilty about doing or not doing something that you cannot show your love? Perhaps you feel guilty because you wish that death would come soon and lift this burden of illness that is too great for all of you. Whatever the feelings, let them be there. Accept them. They are human feelings. Know they are side by side with your love. You would not have these feelings if you did not love this person. These are feelings that happen when you are close to another, bonded, intimate. Feelings of connection are not always as pretty as Hollywood has told us they are. Listen to your feelings. Know them as real, as connected to love.

As you sit there, go behind your upset feelings. See the love that is there. See it sitting in a very clear and quiet place in the very center of your heart, away from all else, just very quietly there, strong and abiding, solid like a diamond, or like an eternal flame. See how this core of love in the very center of your being is untouched by all else that is happening or that will happen. Now see this same place within the heart of your loved one, where this love lives, at the very core of him. See his love untouched by any changes in his body, by the effects of instruments and medications. If your loved one is in a coma, let yourself sense how this core of love is still alive at the center of his being.

Let this core of love in you speak to the core of love in the other. Hear what your core of love says. See what it wants to do. And now, as you sit quietly, hear what the core of love in your loved one says to you. See what it does. Listen. Be very still. Know how abiding it is. See and know how it wants to express itself. Nothing dramatic is necessary. You may be sitting very quietly together. Your core of love may be saying, "You know how much I love you. I'll miss you terribly. I know you are going. I'll never stop loving you." It may be saying nothing. It may be sharing tears. You may be only touching, quietly holding hands. Or listening to a piece of music together. Or looking into each other's eyes. Or combing her hair. Or bathing his feet.

We each have our own special way of expressing our love. We need only listen to our heart to know what that is. As we listen, many tears may flow. Let them be. They are a part of our love. In this short and precious time that is left, come to know that through this quietness and listening to your heart, you can hear your love and hear how it wants to make itself known. This knowledge is in itself a great gift that will go on to be given to those in your life whom you will go on loving.

I forgive,
and I accept
forgiveness.

Forgiveness has always been a profound and problematic ingredient in human existence. It has been a concern of people since ancient times. The mistletoe that we commonly kiss under during the Christmas season was originally gathered at the winter solstice, the darkest time of the year, the time that stirs the dark corners of the soul. The golden bough of mistletoe was held as a symbol of the sun, of life that never dies, not even at the darkest time, when the world seems unforgiven, its light withdrawn. People hung mistletoe over their doorways in order to signal that old enmities and grievances were forgiven.

In the Catholic religion, people periodically go to confession to seek forgiveness. In the Jewish tradition, Yom Kippur is observed each year, during which a person has the opportunity to ask for and to offer forgiveness. On this day, it is said that a person should knock three times on the door of the person he wishes to say he is sorry to. Only after being rebuffed three times should he consider that he has made a full attempt to heal a wound he helped to cause, and only then should he consider that deed annulled.

Why is forgiveness of such importance? In the act of forgiveness, life is cleansed. Until we have forgiven, we cannot let be, we cannot let go, we cannot go on. We remain attached to the past. Sometimes this attachment becomes like a prison:

> Charles did not speak to or see his mother for twenty years. But he thought of her and spoke of her with hatred every day. He dreamed of her, not able to be free even in his sleep. Finally, when she died, he relented and went to her funeral. He did this only at the behest of his friends and family, who knew that it would be harder if he did not take this final chance to connect with his mother, to feel the pain of his life with her. Slowly, afterward, he made peace with her and gained the freedom to go on with his life without bitterness.

Refusal to forgive is a kind of grief that cannot let go because it has not been completed. Just as with all the other aspects of grief, the process of forgiveness cannot be rushed. It has its own rhythm of working through the hatred and hurt that is hidden behind it. One of the reasons that forgiveness is hard to come to is that it covers a well of hurt, of tears, of unfulfilled needs and hopes. In order for us to come to forgiveness, we need to uncover this hurt, feel it, and live through it. It is like a wound that needs to be opened and given to air. The pain itself leads to the healing—and to new hope and new beginnings.

Often, the greatest obstacle to giving the gift of forgiveness is our pride, our fear of losing face, of losing our dignity. After all, don't we lose our dignity if we forgive what has not been fair to us, what has wronged us? Perhaps what this person has done to us violates our basic values, our sense of what is right, of how people should be with one another. Perhaps the person has never given us the apology we feel we deserve. In a way, we may be right. But forgiveness has nothing to do with excusing someone's behavior. Things done that hurt or harm cannot be erased, nor can they always be understood. Then what is forgiveness?

To me, forgiveness is a process in which we long for something more than proving rights and wrongs. We long for a healing of the hurt and hatred that break our spirit. We long for a sense of wholeness. Forgiveness is a process of healing that restores wholeness. We long for something more than our pride. When we let this pride fall away, in our heart of hearts we know that we, too, have wounded others. None of us is above being human, and our awareness of our being good and bad, loving and hating, kind and selfish, caring and hurting brings us a deep dignity, which can never be taken from us. From the humility of knowing how human we are, how imperfect our loving is, comes the dignity of having compassion for ourselves and others. Out of this compassion comes a forgiveness that does not have to do with excusing a wrong or even of understanding it. It is something deeper. It says, "We dwell in the same place, we are clay vessels soon to break, we can only try not to hurt, knowing how precious life is, how fragile we are."

In forgiveness is contained an impulse to sanctify life, to have it begin anew. Imperfect as we are, that is the best we can hope for, to have new beginnings. That is why the mistletoe is hung in the doorway at the darkest time of the year. That is why we are invited to knock three times. These traditions provide for our human frailty—and also for our deepest desire to be free to love and to bless life.

And so we have the cleansing of forgiveness, the cleansing of oneself and of the other.

In the process of forgiveness, we move from anger to hurt, to telling the feelings that hurt, not in order to blame but rather to bare the heart, to be stripped of anger or blame. You may wonder whether someone who is dying can take this. But what a person wants most, it seems to me, is our realness. What I want most in my living is for people to be real with me, not to live any lie with me. I cannot imagine wanting anything other than this realness when I am dying. Real does not mean smiling, kind, peaceful only. Real also means hurt, anger, tears. Real means sharing who I really am. You know the person forgiveness needs to be gone through with. Perhaps he is too ill to engage in this sharing with you. Perhaps no more than a simple, gentle, "I am sorry for . . ." or "I forgive you for . . ." is needed, with a touch or a look that says, "All is cleansed of that wound, all is reconciled between us." Perhaps the two of you cannot outwardly reconcile a hurt. That is all right, too.

You can go through the process of forgiving by yourself. It may take more time than your loved one has to spare with you. Just the wish that is within you will affect the movement of your heart. It will be softer. It will be lighter. Your loved one will know it. Perhaps you will need to forgive yourself for not being as forgiving as you would like to be. It is sometimes hardest to forgive ourselves, to accept that we are less than our ideal. I know a woman who has been berating herself for not holding her husband's hand during the moments of his death. She cannot forgive herself, even though she held his hand in such a loving way throughout their marriage. It is so hard for her to give herself the compassion she would give to anyone else.

Sometimes it takes a long time to go through the process of forgiveness, to oneself or to another. Each of us goes through this journey in our own way and in our own time. You can begin this week. Perhaps you can plant the seed for it by saying, "I want to forgive. I do not yet know how. Please, God, help me to find the way." If you do not pray to God, perhaps you can call upon love, or light or wisdom.

Perhaps you do know the way. What struggle do you need to go through with your pride, or with your sense of what is fair and good? What do you want for yourself that is greater than your pride and your sense of what is right? These are things to wrestle with. What thought, feeling, word, or deed of reconciliation do you long for? You can reflect on this each day. You can write about it in your journal. You can reflect on this theme of forgiveness for the week, seeing what it prompts you toward. And then, after the week, you can let it go, knowing that you have planted the seeds of forgiveness deep within you. They will go on growing, and at some point you will be aware of something stirring you softly or strongly that wants you to do what you must to make life whole.

My heart guides me
to make final
decisions.

The time surrounding the death of someone close to us is like no other time. It is a time that is stark in death's suddenness. Even though dying may have taken a long time, there is the moment in which a curtain separates us from the person who was a part of our lives. It is at this time of sudden and irrevocable turning that we all too often need to make decisions quickly.

Sometimes decisions come very easily during this time. There seems to be some clear crystal voice in our heart that tells us exactly what to do.

As the family gathers around the bed in which a loved one has just died, that crystal voice may say, "I need to be alone with him before the final curtain falls and I leave this room forever." When a heart hears that and can speak it, others may tune in to their needs as well. The family may take turns being alone with the one who is dying or has just died in these intimate last moments of good-bye.

A mother whose child has just died hears that

voice in her heart say, "I want to bring her doll to the funeral home so they can bury it with her. I don't want my child to go off alone. She always takes her doll with her." To the rational mind this may seem like a senseless thing to do, but to the heart of this mother, such a decision guides her in saying good-bye to her child in the way that is true for her. No other voice but the voice of the heart really matters at this moment.

A brother dies suddenly, never having made his wishes for burial arrangements known. The decision must be made as to whether he will be buried or cremated. There is no time for deliberation. The family asks the sister to make this decision, she being closest to her brother.

How shall she do this? She and her brother never spoke of this matter. She does not know his desire. She sleeps on it. The next day, while she sits quietly amid her tears, she hears her heart: "He loved the farm in Vermont. That is where he was happiest. That is the right place to bury him. I think he would want to be cremated, his ashes buried up on the hill. I can't say why, I just feel that he would want that. I will trust that my love for him guides my sense of knowing."

This crystal voice in the center of our heart is really all we ever have as our lightning rod in making any ultimate decision. This voice has nothing to do with right or wrong, with what should or should not be done. In fact, what "should be done" may run totally counter to what we may hear in our hearts. It may sound and seem right, but it will not feel right. This sense of "it does not feel right" is one that we all know well. Often, we say, "If only I had followed that feeling I had, I would have done what I wanted. Next time." But this time there is no next time, and it is our trust in the guidance of our heart that will help us to make decisions we will not regret. Even if someone, friend or family, may later say that things should have been done differently, we can only say, "But this is what my heart told me."

When my father was dying, he had suffered so severe a stroke that there was no chance of his surviving. The doctors wanted to know if I wished to consent to putting him on kidney dialysis so that his life could be prolonged. It was the middle of the night. I was alone with my unconscious father in the emergency room. There was no one to call. No one to consult with. If I told the doctors to stop using any life-support means, my father would be dead by morning.

I left the room and went across the street to the church that was open all night. I went there and sat silently for a long time. No tears. No thoughts, really. No great deliberations. I just sat quietly, silently. Waiting. Waiting for some guidance from deep within my heart. Some voice. Some knowing. Perhaps this is what some people call prayer.

After almost an hour, I felt a clarity within that said, "Let him go. He never wanted to live this way. He never wanted to suffer." Never before had I known the awesome responsibility that love must sometimes carry, the decisions that must sometimes be made in the lonely silence of love.

I went back to the hospital and told the doctors of my decision, so that he could be left in peace to do his leaving. The two doctors at either side of me each put an arm around me, quietly supporting a decision they could not make for me. Then one of the doctors said, "I know how hard this is. I had to make a decision like this for my own father."

Although decisions like this must be made in the depths of aloneness, it helped to have someone reach across the gulf of his aloneness to touch mine. It made my aloneness bearable.

Often decisions do not come easily when they need to be made. We may be too distraught to focus on them. At such times, we may wish to ask someone to take over the decision making, assuring her that we trust her and will honor the decisions that she makes, without later criticism. Perhaps together with her you can make necessary decisions, sitting together and helping each other to hear the voices of your hearts. Perhaps your clergy person, perhaps a hospital social worker, will be available to help you.

During this week, whether the decisions you face are big or small, let yourself simply ask, "What does my heart want? What does my heart need?" Ask this question and then be still. In this stillness, you will hear. You may need to sit quietly for several minutes, or longer. You may hear the voice of your heart in a moment. You may wish to take a long, quiet walk. You will know your best way for listening. And as you follow, you will come to your heart and carry your decisions peaceably.

I complete
unfinished business.

☐

Things we have not finished keep calling to us. We know this in the daily round of our lives. Bills unpaid, letters unwritten, calls unmade have a way of nagging at us until we attend to them. So much more do unfinished things call to us when they are buried in deeper parts of ourselves. These, too, may be small things.

I recall that for months after my father died, I kept getting a bill from the funeral parlor for a death certificate they had provided for me. For months I left these mailings unopened on my desk. I can see now that I did not really want to attend to this little detail, for to have finished this bit of business would have brought a final closing to my father's funeral, and I was not ready to do that. The day I made out the six-dollar check and mailed it, I knew I was ready to close a chapter. All of us hold on to unfinished business in this way so that we can have a small corner where we do not have to say good-bye until we are ready to.

Some corners of unfinished business go much deeper

than these small symbolic acts. These pieces of business take longer to attend to, for the business that needs to be completed cannot be completed with the right person. Death has made that impossible. The door of death has closed with finality on the opportunity to complete things the way we want to. The wife who wanted to hold her husband's hand while he was dying will never be able to. Some of us have the opportunity to hold the hand of a loved one while he is dying, but we are left with something else that cannot be completed in the way we would have desired.

When my father was dying, I stayed the night in his hospital room. I held his hand throughout the night and spoke to him as he lost consciousness and made his passage out of his body. After he died, I left the hospital and went to make the arrangements for his funeral. My father died on a Wednesday, and because funerals are not allowed to be held on the Sabbath in the Jewish religion, I arranged that my father be buried the very next day.

Because I had to make my decision quickly, I did not do something considered essential to the burial of a Jewish man: he was not buried wearing his tallis, the shawl a Jewish man prays in daily and has worn since his Bar Mitzvah at age thirteen. The tallis signifies his commitment to live by the spirit of his religion. My father's tallis was in the drawer of his dresser in another city, and I could not possibly get there in time. The funeral parlor provided one of its prayer shawls for my father, but this shawl did not carry with it all his prayers and pious deeds. Nor did it make up for the fact that I did not honor my father with this final deed of respect. No matter that I had honored him in his illness and in his dying as completely as I could.

This unfinished business stayed with me, wanting me to do something more than feel sadness within my heart. A few months after my father's death, I asked my mother if I could have my father's prayer shawl. Perhaps I could complete unfinished business if I could hold it within my keeping. My mother told me that she had given it to my father's synagogue. And so I went to the rabbi, who showed me the drawer where I could search for it, but all the offered prayer shawls looked alike. I left without even trying to find the right one. It looked as though the business of the prayer shawl would have to be left unfinished forever. But this was not so. Two years after my father's death, I dreamed that I went to the rabbi again to ask him if he had found my father's tallis. In the dream, he said to me, "No, it is finished, your father's prayer shawl. It was finished with his life. You must have your own prayer shawl. Wait. You will. And it will hold the good deeds and prayers of your life."

I thought about the message of this dream for another year. Slowly, the unfinished business of my father's death that had been calling me was unfolding the way of completion to me. The only way for a Jewish woman to receive her own prayer shawl is to be Bat Mitzvahed. If I took the special classes for adults, and was Bat Mitzvahed, I would receive my own tallis, fulfilling my own connection to the spiritual circle of my ancestors. Sometimes unfinished business is completed in mysterious ways, unfolding and inspiring our lives in directions we could not have anticipated and expressing the unbreakable bonds between ourselves and those who are gone.

During this coming week, let yourself consider the unfinished business you wish to complete. Are there small acts, like writing a check, that you can attend to, ready to turn some page of your grief? Is there some deeper form of unfinished business calling to you for completion? Perhaps, like the woman who did not hold her husband's hand, you are sitting with something uncompleted. Some things cannot be completed except with compassionate acceptance of ourselves. Surely this woman will hold someone else's hand in another time and place, in this way completing the need to express her true nature. The heart finds its ways of making peace through completion. Ask your heart this week: What is unfinished for you? What is calling you to do something that will bring you peace, that will bring your loved one peace? Follow whatever it is that calls you, for this is the way of solace and of going on living in a creative way.

I help the child
within me
to say good-bye.

☐

I have a little friend whom I love very much. Her name is Maria. She is three years old. Maria had a special love for my dog, Blue. Blue was frightened of children, but he sensed Maria's special affection and let her hold his leash on our walks to the meadow. I would sit under the apple tree and watch them run gleefully. At night, on the telephone, Maria and I had our Blue ritual. "Where is Blue-Blue?" she would ask. I would say, "Blue-Blue is sleeping now, but he sends you a kiss," and I would send it for him through the phone.

Last spring, when Blue let me know with his tender eyes that he was ready to go after so long an illness, I wrapped him in his blanket and took him to the vet to be put to sleep. I held him while he slowly relaxed and left his little body, letting silence surround us. I kissed him good-bye and left.

That night, Maria got on the phone and said, "I know, Blue-Blue went to heaven. But where is he? Is he sleeping? Where's my kiss?" Maria spent many months trying to figure death and Blue out, but it was all beyond her. Burying his ashes under the apple tree, planting flowers over them —none of this really helped. Maria still asked, "Where is Blue-Blue?" Until she stopped asking and Blue just seemed to disappear for her.

One cold December day, Maria and I went for a walk in the meadow and stopped at the apple tree. Growing out of the ground was one small red bud. Maria ran to it, kissed it, and said, "Oh, look! Blue sent me a flower." To myself I said, Yes, maybe he did.

There is this child in all of us, still trying to fathom someone being here, being gone, coming back, not coming back. It is as if we are still playing those old hide-and-seek games that children love to play so that they can master the comings and goings, know that when something is gone it can come back. But then there are those childhood losses when those who have gone cannot be brought back just by removing our hands from our eyes. Grandparents die, parents separate, dear friends move, dogs or cats die. These early separations make profound impressions on the soul of a young child and color our adult reactions to loss.

A young woman said to me: "When I was in kindergarten my parents separated. My mother and I moved very suddenly. It's strange, but all I can remember before that is having made butter in kindergarten class. I remember carrying it home in a little bowl. It shone in my hands just like the sun, warm and golden, and I had made it myself.

"Everything went dark after that and I could not bring the sun back. I used to walk through the streets calling out for my father, but I couldn't bring him back."

As an adult, Debra experienced the deaths of

those she loved as echoes of that early experience of abandonment. With each loss she fell through a crack right into the darkness of her childhood.

What Debra and I did together, you can do. We went to see her inner child, to talk to her, to help and heal her. You can do the same: Let yourself relax. Loosen any restrictive clothing. Close your eyes. Listen to your breathing. You may wish to play some quiet music. Let yourself drift... until you approach the child within you who is feeling abandoned or desolate or afraid to be left alone. See this child, and hear what it says. Debra's child said, "Please don't leave me. Who will hold me at night? I'm afraid to be alone. I'm afraid of the dark. Are you leaving me because I did something bad?" What does your child say? Take the time to listen. Be with this child. Hold it. Let it cry or be angry, whatever it needs to share with you. Don't judge this child. Accept it. Let it be. When children can be who they are, can feel and share what they are feeling, they feel held and whole. Give this to yourself.

And then let your grownup self speak to your child self with all of the wisdom of your years, your experience, with all that you are now that that child couldn't possibly be expected to have been. Let yourself help this child. This is what Debra said to her child self:

> Dear, dear child, this is not the same. This is not the same as your daddy's not being here. This is a different kind of leaving. Poor Debra, you missed your father so much. You felt he left because you were bad. But that was not so. And Mike (her husband) is leaving now, but not because you are bad. Death is different. Mike had to go. It was time for him to go. And you know, you can always carry him

with you. People die, people go. I know death is
hard for you to understand. It will take time. But let's
say good-bye to Mike. Let's let him go to wherever
he is going. Let's tell him we love him and bless him
on his journey.

What do you say to your child self? This week, each
day spend a few moments, or longer, with your child. Go
to it. Listen to it. Give it what it needs. As you do this, you
are healing not only the present. You are healing the
wounds of the past as well.

I may want to express something personal at the memorial or funeral service.

All too often as we sit at a memorial service, we listen to a clergy person speak about the one who has just died and we sense a hollowness in what is being said. The person may be kindly, but if he has not known the one he is eulogizing, he cannot possibly convey the essence of that person. Such moments leave us feeling a sense of hollowness within ourselves, a loneliness over and beyond the aloneness we feel in our grief, for our deep sense of the person we have lost is not being reflected to us.

There are times when we cannot ourselves muster the spiritual strength to stand up and say what is in our heart. We can, however, sit quietly in privacy with the clergy person who is to speak at the service. We can share openly our precious thoughts about this loved one who has gone. I recall doing this with the person who eulogized my daughter. I could not speak at the service—I was too broken, too dazed even to think of gathering myself to stand before people. I needed just to sit quietly at that service. But I can still recall sitting with that clergy person in the twilight of his office, talking about my daughter, sharing little things about her that were precious to me.

I told him about something she had said to me just days before she got sick, to explain why someone she loved was crying. She said, "Maybe the flashes, the splashes, the sprays of sand in his eye made him cry." That was a gem of a memory to me, the way a child could speak a poem. I told him things like this. And as he spoke at the service, he presented all that I had said, had woven it into some tapestry of my daughter's short life that brought great solace to me. He later mailed a typed copy of that talk to me, and even today, twenty years later, I sometimes find myself reading those pages, still feeling the sense of solace that I felt then.

I recall, too, that I had asked a friend of mine to play a particular piece of piano music by Bach. We sat quietly, all of us together in the comfort that sometimes only music can bring, bathing us all in healing. And so, even though I could not take an active role on this occasion, I told people what was important to me, what I needed for comfort and for meaning. We can do this. Those who surround us at this time can create a circle of solace for us.

Many people think that they must follow some very traditional funeral ritual. Perhaps that is true if you belong to a particular religious community. Such a service may, in fact, be what brings you your particular solace. You may also want to experience a more personal sharing and can do this in addition to your traditional service. You can gather together those closest to you, perhaps in your living room, and read something, say something, listen to some music that the deceased loved.

Sometimes we find that it is important to participate actively in a service. When my friend Nina died, we held a memorial service in which everyone who wished to was able to speak about her. After minutes of silent meditation, people spoke: a memory, a feeling, something sad, something funny. People just spoke as their heart moved them. One person would finish, and out of the silence another would begin, stringing together a necklace of memory and love. We all felt Nina's presence in the room. We felt that that was the way she would have wanted it. We sang, too. We sang "Amazing Grace" with tears and smiles.

It is in these times of loss that we most need to create something in which we have ourselves, our love, our life force. These form the bridge to those who are gone. At these moments when we least have ourselves, we somehow must find the strength to be ourselves. This is the only way we can carry a light in this darkest of times. It is the light of our own life spark that goes on, even in the darkest time, raising up the spirit of the one who is gone. In this way, through our love, through our light, even at a memorial service, even at a funeral, there is something present of the one who is gone—present in our love, in our tears, in our smiles, as we give expression to our loss in our own personal way.

This week, let yourself reflect on what this memorial or funeral service needs to be for you. Do you need to take a more active role? Writing something? Reading something? Whatever you need to do is fine. There is no right way. There is only your way.

I help the child
within me
attend the service
and funeral.

Laura is a woman in her forties. She was seven when her father died. He had been ill for some time, but this was no obstacle to the closeness between father and daughter. When he became so ill that he had to be hospitalized, he reassured his daughter that he would return soon and asked her to write a little story that she could read to him when he returned home. Laura's mother spent much time at the hospital. One day when she returned home, Laura watched her approach the house with her head bent, her face tear-stained, her arms supported by Laura's uncles. She did not ask, but slowly she came to understand that her father had died, that he would not be coming home to hear the story she had been writing for him.

When Laura looks back at that time, she can see that something froze within her then. She never cried, she never asked what had happened to her father. She never witnessed any part of his death. She never attended his funeral. Silence filled in the empty spaces, an icy silence that froze her grief into forgetfulness. Laura's grief for her

45

father remained under the ice; the child within her had been frozen there. Laura relived her loss in a different way. She went to the past and relived her father's death in a way that would not freeze a child.

She went to the hospital. Her father held her hand, said good-bye to her, told her he loved her. She cried with him, told him she loved him. She asked him the questions that children need to ask. No, he was not going because she was a bad girl. She was good, she was special. She was wonderful. She read her little story to him. She went to the funeral, felt her mother's arm around her, her little brother's hand in hers. She felt the togetherness of her family sharing its grief. She felt her tears, and there was no need for them to freeze. For the first time, she cried the tears she could not cry as a child.

Laura took her father's ashes that she always carried within her. She carried them and planted them in the earth now. A rosebush grew, flowers of new life, risen out of the ashes. She completed the story of her childhood grief. She wept soft tears. She became a softer person, able to open a heart that was no longer frozen.

No matter what age we are, each of us who loses a loved one has such a child within us. This inner child has as much need to be supported in its grief as do the children outside of us. The same considerations need to be given to both. All too often we are more attentive to providing for the needs of little children at the time of a death, more attentive than Laura's family was able to be. The same guidelines apply to both the inner and the outer child. What does the child need?

The child needs to be opened to the truth of what is happening. The child needs to express its feelings, to ask questions, to be held, to feel contact, to share tears and memories. The child needs to be able to say it is angry, sad, confused, alone. The child needs to be able to be a part of all that is being shared by the family, to feel surrounded by contact and warmth even if the warmth is sad. There is nothing as chilling, as icy, as feeling alone at such a time, as sensing but not really knowing what is going on.

This week, be aware of the child within you. Do not leave it alone in an inner icy silence. Sit with it, hear its voice, ask it what it needs. Does it need to sit beside someone at the service who is especially comforting to it? Does it need to share something at the funeral? Does it need just to be quiet beside someone? Does it need to ask someone to come along who might not otherwise be there, but who would be there just for this child? Perhaps a friend, even someone who did not know the deceased.

Spend time with your inner child. Perhaps she thinks she must go to the service but secretly wishes not to. Let yourself listen to all these feelings. Perhaps it is right for you not to go. It is only by listening that you will know. Perhaps it is enough for the inner child merely to express these feelings, to know that it is all right to have such feelings. Often, just to express them frees us to take the next step. Perhaps you can share these feelings with someone so that you are not alone, just so that you can flow softly through this time, helping the child within you to live through this part of its grief.

Rituals can help me.

The rituals that surround the death of someone we love can be very healing for us. The problem is that in our day and age, ritual is too often routinized. Funeral services are usually sterile, the person making the eulogy more often than not does not know the person he is eulogizing. But if we give our heart's attention to the rituals we need, we can create the sacred time and space in which to say good-bye to a loved one. Through ritual, we create a sacred circle in which to let our love as well as our tears flow.

The ritual of farewell can begin at the bedside of the person who is dying. Sitting quietly together forming a circle that holds the dying person in love is a ritual that offers solace to everyone present. The rituals of the religious traditions we grew up in can offer profound solace for those who are bereaved. It is helpful if the person guiding the ritual knows the deceased, or if someone close to the deceased can sit with that person and let flow from the heart the words that will tell of the essence of that person.

When my daughter died, I wanted her to be cremated. I could not deal with picturing her under the earth. But her grandfather wept and said, "But where will I visit her?" And so she was buried. I never went to the funeral. I couldn't. I stayed at home with a friend. Sometime later, I had my own ritual of planting a garden. Now, as I look back, I believe that had I been able to participate in the ritual of my daughter's burial, I would have been better able to say good-bye, to let her go sooner. Since that time, when loved ones have died, I go to the burial. I step forward, take the shovel, place earth down to cover the coffin. In this way I say good-bye to the ones I love, I bless their going with love, I see their bodies in the earth, returned to dust, and I see their spirits released into the light. Participating in the ritual helps me to participate in reality, to let go, to say good-bye.

Rituals put us in touch, put us in the circle in which we open ourselves to be touched, in which we may touch the dead one, touch the earth. In our participation, we are not only confronting death, we are also honoring life. We are touching the source of life and death, which is our open presence in the living moment.

This is a description of a ritual in which my friend Nina's ashes were buried:

After a quiet lunch we walked to the top of the hill. Herb carried the urn. Jess brought the shovel and the pick. When we got to the apple trees, Jess and Judd began to dig a hole in front of the rock covered with green moss between the two apple trees. We then gathered around the hole. Herb opened the urn and handed it to Nina's older son, Judd. He poured the ashes into the hole. We were all silent, each alone with our thoughts of Nina, still not believing that she

was gone. We each filled the hole with earth, and
Herb placed a small rock on top. We each said good-
bye to her. We picked some wildflowers and placed
them on the rock, and Jess found a four-leaf clover
and went back up the hill to put that on the stone,
too. Then we went back to the house and had tea.
Judd put on a Vivaldi record.

This is a ritual created together by those who loved
Nina, who had never made her burial desires known. If
your loved one has, then the ritual will be known to you. If
not, you will need to listen to your heart, as we listened to
ours, in order to create your own ritual.

During this week, sit with those who are closest to your
loved one who is dying or has died. Share what ritual each
of you feels will most reflect your love and the essence of
the one who has just gone. Know that together you can
create the ritual that carries what is true for all of you.
And, too, if you write about your participation in this ritual, write it in detail in your journal, so that you will have
it there to look back upon in quiet moments of reflection.

Death teaches me
about letting go.

Imagine that you are sitting in front of a movie screen. Look at the blank white screen. See the title of the movie appear on the screen. It is called *Letting Go*. It is your movie.

What are the pictures you see on the screen? What are the images of letting go? Do you see yourself holding on and crying out, "Don't go, don't go, please don't go," and then, knowing that the other is going, letting go but still in some way refusing to let go? Or do you see yourself letting go with acceptance, with love? Or do you see yourself at a mountain meadow, holding a bird or a kite and letting it go so that it can fly away? Can you feel that moment of not wanting to let go of this lovely kite, this lovely bird, this loved one—and then the moment of shifting, the release into letting go, knowing that it is time for this bird, this kite, this beloved soul to spread its wings and move on? Or do you see yourself letting go into singing loudly or crying deeply, or into making love? It is striking to see how these words—"letting go"—have a twofold meaning: releasing in the sense of letting go of someone or something, and in the sense of releasing into, letting be, being yourself. In both of these senses of "letting go," the same thing is necessary, and that is a trust in the process of life, in the universe.

I knew a little boy. When he was about five years old, he was very preoccupied with the moon. He would watch it wax and wane from his window each night. He was fine when the moon was new, but as it grew to full he grew more and more anxious. He was afraid that the moon, which he believed was made of white shiny stone, would be so big and so heavy that it would fall to earth and destroy things and hurt him and his mommy and daddy. Perhaps this little boy was trying to say that he didn't feel very safe in the world of grownups and big things. Perhaps, too, he was feeling something of the mystery of the universe. Perhaps he was trying to figure things out as he looked out of his window each night, just as the earliest people must have looked up into the vast universe and tried to understand the mysteries that surrounded them. What makes the moon come and go? What makes life come and go? Sometimes it is so awesome that we feel the immensity of the mystery will crush us.

Some of us try to deal with the insecurity of living in a universe that we cannot fathom or control by controlling ourselves—our feelings, our time, our money, our children, our thoughts, our stories. And then, just when we think we have everything under control, death rises into our lives, in all of its fullness, just like the full moon that terrified the little boy. And once again we come face-to-face with our insecurity, with the limits of our control, with the need to let go. Death teaches us that change is the law of life. Death is the big teacher, but there are smaller "deaths" that also teach us about letting go: the loss of a job, of a love affair, of our youth, of some dream that we couldn't make come true.

Nothing can be held on to. But change does have its own law. The moon's phases are predictable, as are those of the seasons of the year and of life. Yes, there are exceptions. Children do die young. There are natural disasters like earthquakes and floods. But for the most part, life has predictable seasons and cycles. We may not like them. We may rebel against them. But when we let go into these changes, the insecurity of being alive can begin to dissipate, and we can begin to find a resting place.

A young mother I know recently became pregnant with her third child. She had not planned for this pregnancy and was very disappointed. She had just begun to work in a hospice for terminally ill people and was very involved in helping them in their dying process. She and her husband decided to have this child. She sat with me and shared:

> I am sad not to be doing the hospice work just now. But I can't. I'm so nauseated that I can't do anything right now. But I am very aware that I am doing just the same thing that the people dying in the hospice must do. I do not really want this pregnancy, but because of my respect for this life, I accept it. Just as they must accept dying. I cannot do anything about the nausea. The more I fight it, the worse it will be. I just have to let go into it. And I will get bigger and bigger. Just like the moon. I will become full and heavy and filled with light. It will just happen within me. Just as death is happening within the people at the hospice. So, they and I are learning the same lesson. Letting go into pregnancy, into childbirth, and letting go into death are the same thing.

This young mother had somehow become aware of the underlying order of the universe and of how she is a part of it, that its laws apply to her, to birthing and living and dying. She had somehow learned that it is the very fighting against the process that would cause her to suffer.

In our society, there are so many ways in which people deny death, try to control change, and refuse to let go into it. Women, and more and more men, "make up" for graying hair, try to stay young, look young, undo change. Even the corpse is "made up" to look young, actually wearing makeup. How sad, not to be able to take our last look at the plain, real, true face of our loved one. How sad, to be so frightened of letting go into death, of needing to control, that we cannot have the chance to look into the face of death and see that it is not as terrible as we feared. Perhaps not terrible at all. Perhaps peaceful, still, finally letting go, the spirit free like the lovely kite, like the bird, releasing.

This week, ask yourself, Am I still holding on to the dying or the dead? Why won't I let go? See yourself sitting once again in front of the movie screen. On the screen, see the picture of yourself holding on, and then watch the screen, watch the movie going on. See the scene shifting. See yourself letting go. See what you are doing, saying, accepting as you let go. See the movie through to the end. Ask yourself if there is any way you can carry what you saw on the screen into your life. Is it anger that you need to let go of? Or some feeling of guilt? Remember that into the space that opens when we let go, something else arises. Know for yourself what moves in as you let go. It may be sadness or patience or compassion, tears, or similar forms of release. Whatever it is, let it come. Welcome it as your life.

I take the time
to be with my loss.

□

Our obligations pull at us. Work, family, promises we have made to others, all make us feel indispensable. All too often, these obligations take us back into a stream of hectic activity and prevent us from living with the loss we have just had. In giving up the time to be with this loss, we give something up that we can never have in quite the same way again.

Sometimes we give up this time because we are afraid to have it, to feel too much, to be quiet, to digest our feelings. But this is a mistake, for the days following the loss of someone we love are like no other time. In these days are the possibilities of letting yourself absorb your loss, of journeying through it. It is only by going through a door that we come out the other side. It is only by going through darkness that we reach the light. It is only through tears that we come toward smiles. If we rush right back to our accustomed routines, we cut off this process.

The fact is that we are not indispensable. Those who are part of our world will go on with things as we take the time to be with our loss. In the Jewish tradition, it is customary to take seven days after the funeral during which we refrain from our daily chores. We do not work. We do not cook or shop. We separate ourselves from our daily habits in order to be able to be with our feelings of grief without distraction. Some people feel the need to take time and go to a distant place where they can leave behind everything that is familiar.

After losses that have been deep for me, I have found it most healing to spend time with a friend who lives in a distant city. There, comfort is present for me in the form of friendship. I am free to be with myself, not having to care for things at home. It is also a comfort to me to go somewhere where nature is healing, where I can walk long stretches by myself, where there is the space to stop, to sit and cry, to write in my journal, to lie on the grass and look up at the vast sky and wonder into the emptiness. Nature is my place of finding myself, of letting myself be, of letting myself go.

What is your place? What do you need during these days when loss surrounds you both inside and out? For each person it is different. I know those who want to be at home, where doing the ordinary things brings comfort. Making a cup of tea, sipping it while sitting quietly. Working alone in the garden, touching the earth, pulling weeds, tending life. Making a quiet dinner or making no dinner at all. Being close to the space you shared with the person who is there no more. Feeling the empty space. Being touched by it. By the silence. By the finality. Not believing it. She must be coming back. No. And silence again. The stark nakedness of this loss. All to be felt. All to be lived with. Time to feel the sorrow, the bewilderment, the terror, the tenderness. Time to sit with close ones. To reminisce. To cry together. To eat quietly together. To wonder, What next? What now? How is it possible to go on? Perhaps the time to share feelings of relief that suffering is over. The time to walk through rooms and touch things that belonged to someone and now belong to no one. To touch no-moreness.

This space of no-more is a transitional space, like a corridor, like the silence between two notes of music. That is why I call it an empty space, this space between she-was-here and she-is-gone. If we stay in this space, if we let ourselves be in it, something comes through it. It may be our tiredness, and so we sleep. It may be unfinished things we hear spoken inside, and so we write in our journal. It may be wrenching sorrow, and so we cry. It may be feelings of poignant tenderness, and so we need to touch something, someone. It may be anger, and so we rage. Whatever it is, we can only go past our grief if we take this transitional time to be with it.

What do you need to do with this time? How much time do you need? Where do you need to be and with whom? Sometimes you plan before a death for these days. Sometimes you cannot know until the time of loss comes. Try truly to listen to yourself, to what you really need.

Martha, whose mother has been dying of cancer for some time, told me, "I have been grieving for months. I will be so relieved when my mother dies. It has been so terrible for her and such a strain on all of us. After the funeral, I just want to go home. I don't want to be together with my relatives, to receive condolence calls. This is just not a time for me to do that. I just need to be quietly at home, going through my mother's things. I've spent so much of my life doing what others think is right. I don't want to do that at such an important time as this. I need to be true to myself so that I can really go through my mother's death."

As you listen to yourself, you will know what you need on this path of bereavement. You will know what turns to take. You will know how and where to rest with your loss so that you can move on when it is time.

I deal
with the belongings
that are left.

The belongings that are left behind by a loved one are filled with both the life and the loss of that person. They stand around us heavy with memory, with feeling, and they stand empty, without their owner. They reflect the emptiness we feel back to us. We and they are bereft of a living presence. We are like these objects: alone, uprooted, somewhere and somehow in between and disconnected, waiting for the time when we will know where we belong, where to set down new roots, where and with whom we will have new connection, new meaning. Meanwhile, we feel suspended in time and space just like the clothing, the books, the little things, the toothbrush, the bathrobe and slippers.

And so it is that the process of our dealing with these things becomes very important for us. As we let go of the belongings that seem to contain the life of the one we have lost, we are letting go of that person in a very tangible way. Some of us want to let go of everything very quickly, clean things out, send them to the Salvation Army. We may prefer to have someone else do the job so that we do not have to face the painful feelings that come with the process of letting go. If so, our family and friends can be of great help to us, lifting a burden that feels too heavy for us.

Whenever it is possible, however, for us to go through the belongings of our loved one, it is wise to do so, because in this process there is a healing. It may take time to approach these belongings. It may take days, or weeks, or even months. That is all right. Going through belongings in order to let go is a very personal experience. There are things that can be sorted out and given away very quickly.

Laura asked a relative to sort out her deceased mother's underwear and toiletries and other neutral belongings. She asked that the clothing and hats her mother had made be saved for her to go through herself. She knew that she would need time in order to be with these clothes. She waited several months until she was ready. She spent time with a close friend by her side deciding what to do with these things that her mother had put so much of herself into. She could feel her mother's life in these things. She wept as she sorted them out, saying good-bye to her mother just a little further.

Just a little further, just a little more of letting go as we part with the belongings of a loved one. We may find ourselves holding on to things that somehow hold special meaning to us. We may keep ourselves surrounded by these things, letting go of them just a little more as time goes by.

Sally kept her husband's warm sweater that was torn at the elbows. For a long time, she wore it whenever it got cold in the house. She felt her husband's warmth around her each time she put it on. And then one day, a year or so later, she just stopped wearing it. She had let go. She had absorbed his warmth into her. It was a part of her. She mended the holes at the elbows and gave it to a shelter for homeless men. She could not have given the sweater away any sooner.

And so it is with all the belongings of a beloved. One day we just realize that something we have been holding on to for a long time is just there, around us, without our needing it or even wanting it. Time to let it go, for it has already helped us go through our grief.

Over time, we may find that there is just one thing that we need to keep, something that becomes a symbol of our love and our memory of a loved one. For me, it is my daughter's little red Mexican chair, which stands in a corner of the room. Little children love to sit in it when they visit. And my father's gold coin that he carried for good luck since the Depression days. And a cup that my friend Nina made for me. I sometimes will drink a cup of tea from it when I need to feel soothed. All the other things have dropped away, fallen into oblivion, no longer needed. Love holds itself in my heart without needing any longer to be held by outer things. But with some things it has taken a very long time to let go. My daughter's little yellow toothbrush stayed in the toothbrush holder for a good ten years after I had let all else go. Letting go of that took an afternoon of being home alone, feeling an old ache reawaken in my chest, feeling tears, and then quietly taking the toothbrush and throwing it away. Time is there for us to dwell in until solace comes to offer us the gift of letting go slowly, making space within ourselves for new life to enter.

During this week, consider how you need to go about letting go of the belongings of your loved one. Do you need help from family? From friends? Who will be most comforting to have near you? To talk things over with about how you wish to proceed? To help you sort things

out? To do part of the job for you? When is it right for you
to begin to deal with these things? Your timing needs to
come from within you, from what feels right and comfortable and comforting for you. Let yourself feel your way,
knowing just how this can best be a healing and meaningful experience for you.

I may feel numbness
as part of my grief.

How is it possible that everything around me looks the same when I feel that things will never be the same again? Everything seems to be in its fixed place. The clock is still going. The geranium on the windowsill is still a brilliant red. My child still calls, "Mommy." Morning still comes and so does night. How can everything still be the same when the whole universe seems to have shifted for me? My eyes squint and my brow furrows, as I try to understand. But this cannot be understood. It is all beyond understanding. Bewilderment and numbness are felt in this silent din of confusion.

It is the kind of numbness that protects us from things we cannot understand, from things that are too painful. It is like needing to shield our eyes from a naked, blinding sun. We cannot really look at that sun without some protection. For most of us this protection is our illusion that our own lives and the lives of those we love will keep going on. Now, in grief, we are looking at the sun without any shield. And so we need our numbness to shield us until we grow used to the glare of death without illusion. The days that we take to be with our loss can provide us with time and space to be with this numbness and to let it soften as we get used to the naked sun. Not that this numbness will necessarily wear away after a few days or even a few weeks. For some it takes more time.

In part, the numbness protects us from feelings that we fear may be too powerful; it allows them to come through to us slowly so that we can absorb them. It is like an emotional digestive process. During the days immediately after our loss, and during the days and weeks and months that follow, the times in which we are quiet allow us to feel what is just under this numbness. You may find your hand resting on your chest or softly stroking your arm. You can take the time to feel what your hand is doing. Perhaps it is touching those feelings just below the thin ice of numbness. This is why quiet moments are so important. It is important to be with yourself. To give yourself the time to return.

In numbness there is also the sense that we, too, have departed. There is a feeling of deadness. Perhaps that is true, in some way. When our world is no longer the same, when our familiarity with a loved one is shattered by death, it is as if the me I know is no longer. The me I have known in relation to this intimate other is shattered. Part of my numbness is this sense of my loss of myself. That is why so many people say, "A part of me has gone with him." Without that person it is as if the geography of a journey has been changed and we are left in a strange land.

It takes time to find a new compass within oneself. It takes time to find one's footing on the ground of one's everyday life again, slowly to find one's way back into routines as one comes alive again. During this period of returning to ourselves, friends and family members are very important. They are our familiar landmarks. To see and touch them and be touched by them gives us solid ground again. Some balanced rhythm of company and quietness helps us. Company so that we know we are not alone. And quietness because we are alone.

It is during our times alone that we begin to reach what is below the numbness. Walking her dog alone at night, Laura looks out at the dark velvet sky. Suddenly she is crying. A moment before she had not felt any tears. When she is alone, they come. Being alone is not the same as loneliness. It is a solitude, a coming to oneself, slowly lifting your numbness, your curtain of grief. Eve sits at night knitting and listening to music, after everyone is asleep. As she knits, she lets her heart be quiet, she hears her fear at being alone. Even though she is a grown woman, a mother, in this quietness, after everyone else has gone to bed, she can hear below the numbness. She can hear the little girl in her. She listens. She feels less numb.

You can do the same. You can make time to be with your numbness. To touch it. To hear what is beneath it. To touch and listen slowly. To know that time will melt this feeling of no-feeling.

I welcome
the consolation
of family and friends.

The vigil you have spent with the dying is over. The one close and dear to you has died. His or her physical presence is gone. It is over. There is a gaping emptiness. A cut has taken place in the bond that connected the two of you, as surely as if it were a physical cut. You may actually feel this cut in your chest or solar plexus or stomach. Even though you know that the bond of the spirit may never be cut, the cut that does take place hurts terribly.

In this time of being cut from the cord of life that joined living to living, we feel more acutely than at any other time the sense of stark aloneness. We feel like a "motherless child," like a childless mother, like a husbandless wife, as if a part of ourselves had been amputated, because in a very real way it has. At this time, when we feel small and stunned and bereft, it is the instinct of those who go on living and who go on loving us to gather around us, to enfold us in their comfort. They gather around us to kindle light and warmth in the sudden darkness that has encircled our soul. They gather to comfort us, to touch the aloneness, to encircle us with life.

Most often, after the funeral service, this purest of instincts is expressed in the ritual of the "condolence call," during which you sit at home with the closest family and receive visitors. This time is usually filled with lots of talk and food. Do not feel that you have to join in the talk. Just sitting with those who are talking can be comforting. Know that you can be there quietly. In the Jewish tradition, visitors are not even supposed to say hello to the mourner when they enter the house, in order not to burden him with needing to say hello in return. And so, let yourself be greeted quietly. Feel free to sit in silence, to speak when you feel like it, to ask for food or drink when you need it, to leave and go to your room if you wish to, to ask someone to take a quiet walk with you. Whatever it is, let this be your time to follow your heart, to receive the comfort of others in a way that is really true to yourself.

Sometimes, too, it may be your heart's need to say, "No, thank you." This is not a time to worry about being polite to people. If they are truly caring, they will know that what matters most now, what is most healing, is that you say yes to your own real needs.

When Alex's mother died, his many friends called and visited and took for granted that he would want to talk about his feelings and memories of his mother. But this was not what Alex needed. His real need was just to be with his friends, to talk about "little nothings," to be soothed by the ordinariness of just being together. He told this to his friends and they understood. As they just sat or just walked and just talked together, Alex slowly began to tell this or that about his mother's life and death.

Alex followed the way of his heart, and his friends and

family took the loving lead. Consolation is this kind of dance, and every dance is different, led by the true needs of the mourner and followed by the loving hearts of those who are there to care. When someone close to us dies, most often we spend a week or more together with our family, staying close to comfort one another and to attend to practical matters. During this period, ask yourself, in the quietness of your own heart, if you are receiving what you need. Do not let your needs become lost in the shuffle of family activities. These activities can be very comforting as they provide very needed contact. And yet they can distract and dull us to what we need deep within.

Take a few minutes in the early morning when you awake and can most easily find some time alone. Sit quietly. Ask yourself, What do I need today? With whom do I need to spend some special time? Is there something special I need to do? Let yourself know, for these are the days when your heart can be very receptive to knowing what really needs to happen within yourself and between you and others.

After Jane's father died, she felt a very strong need to be at the beach, to feel the clean ocean air and hear the sounds of the waves. She needed to sit on a stretch of open beach. She needed to have the open space to weep into and to quietly talk to her father in.

She didn't know how she could do this, because her family was gathered together at her mother's house. She felt obligated to be there, and a part of her truly wanted to be with them all. But as she quietly sat with herself, she heard her heart's true need and knew that this was the only way in which she could complete saying good-bye to her father.

Jane told her closest friend of her need and together they sat with and told Jane's family. The family understood, and Jane went off for three days to
the beach with her friend. There she did what she had
to do and then left the beach peacefully to return to
the family, able to be with them and to have them be
with her—fully and with an open heart.

Some of us, after being with our family, will return to
our own home with some feeling that we still need to be
together in a certain way with certain people, in order to
touch some deep inner place in us that is asking for consolation.

When my father died, I returned home after being
with my family and felt a need to be with a few of
my closest friends. I invited them to be with me during an evening. Each of my friends brought a small
and simple food offering. We sat very quietly around
the candlelit table. My friends knew how much this
quiet, simple gathering meant to me upon my return
home, how much it helped to root me back into my
everyday world. Then we sat together and each of us
said a little bit of what my father meant to us, each
one adding their words of consolation that I could
hold close to my heart.

Ask yourself if there is something you may need after
your family gathering has stopped, after the large or small
stream of visitors has slowed, after the first days of mourning have passed and you can better and more slowly listen
to your heart's needs. Know the consolation you need to

receive and let yourself receive it. The word "console" means "comfort together." What more can we do in the face of death than to affirm the presence of the bond of comfort among the living and to pray for those in this world who lack this blessing and who mourn alone.

I live through
the long nights.

It is night. Everyone in the house has gone to sleep. Or if you live alone, everyone you know is out there beyond your reach, for they, too, are probably asleep. There is only the silence surrounding you. The silence and the dark of night. You may hear an occasional car go by. An occasional creaking sound of something, someone, moving somewhere. And then silence again. The silence seems endless, as if the night will go on forever. That is what makes the nights of grief so unbearable.

In this silence, in the absence of all distraction, the pain of grief opens. There seems to be no solace, no one to be comforting, no contact. In this time we realize how the mere physical presence of others is in itself a comfort: the storekeeper who says hello, the bus driver, the person beside us as we wait for the green light. The comfort of human presence sustains and anchors us in the flow of life. But in the night, when someone has gone away, never to return, our aloneness and the pain of our loss seem so endless that we feel we will never get through it. When people were with us earlier in the day, we may even have felt a dullness, a wish to be alone, but now that we are alone, we want people around us and wonder if morning will ever come.

As we live through these nights, through the depths of our aloneness, we discover many things. We discover ways of comfort, of solace, that we never knew of before. The making of a cup of tea can become a comfort. Holding the warmth of the cup as we sit in silence after a long time of tossing and turning in bed. Sitting, walking about, sitting, waiting for the first light of dawn, learning how to be with a hurting self. After weeks, perhaps months, beginning to crochet or knit the squares of an afghan, one square a night, and on some nights two because it took so long to get through it. Finally stitching the squares of aloneness into a blanket of warmth for oneself. Finding a way, if the nights get too long, of bringing contact toward oneself. Falling asleep as the light comes up, knowing a friend or relative will call when she awakens. Or beginning to take walks at dawn, feeling the softness of the new day beginning. Allowing tears through the night. Allowing the muteness of the heart that feels as mute, as endlessly dark as the night. Learning that we can be in and survive dark and alone and broken places. Learning that through the darkest darkness, new light comes.

It does not matter whether we live with a large family or alone, for it is in our aloneness that we go through these nights. It is in this aloneness that we confront our loss. It is in this aloneness that we begin to reckon with the ultimate reality of our aloneness. This is why the nights are often nights of terror for us. We meet with terror the starkness of our aloneness as we never have before.

Some of us are reminded of being afraid of the dark when we were children. We called for our mother or father and feared no one would come. And here we are, thrown back again on this terror. Only now we are not children. Even though there is a child within us, there is also the adult who can hold this child, who knows more and can take this child through the dark nights.

Ellen's husband died in his mid-fifties. They had had a very happy marriage. They were looking forward to his retirement, saving as much as they could so that they would be able to take a year traveling. Then Harold got colon cancer and they had to use their savings to travel to Europe to see a doctor. Months after returning home, Harold died.

Ellen was left with broken dreams, bereft of the husband she loved and had so many plans with. She had never imagined living without him before they became old.

Ellen's nights were the hardest. She thought of committing suicide. She did not think she could get through her grief. For nearly a year she stayed awake at night and took a nap during the day.

Slowly, she began to write in her journal during the night. She wrote of her memories for her grandchildren. She began to include photos in this book. She wanted these youngsters to know the lives of their grandparents. Out of the anguished nights came a beautiful tribute to her life with her husband, a beautiful gift to her grandchildren and great-grandchildren.

Out of the dark night, our soul gives birth to something new. We come to learn about the healing qualities of solitude. We learn that in the darkness there can grow a part of us that we never knew before. A quiet center, a place that we come to feel as an inner home. In this solitude, a new light is kindled. It is a mystery how this light comes, a light more tender, more poignant, more precious than any light we have known before. With it we are more able to sweep darkness away, able to hold our light to ourselves, to others, and to life.

During this week, allow yourself to follow your heart toward what might truly give you comfort through these nights. Let yourself seek the comfort you need. Talk with a loved one about what you need. Write in your journal. Take time during the day to reflect on what you need now to take you through the nights. If they are too difficult to get through on your own right now, perhaps you may speak with your clergy person or with a bereavement counselor referred by your family physician. With help and comfort, you will find your way, your particular way of solace, toward the healing strength of your solitude.

Guilt and remorse
may be part
of my grief.

Bill's mother died five years ago. He still feels guilty that he did not have more love for her when she was alive.

Linda tells me that after her son died of leukemia at age eighteen, she felt guilty that she had not allowed him to drive cross country with friends after his graduation from high school. She could not forgive herself that she had denied him what would have been a last pleasure.

I feel guilty that I did not bury my father with his prayer shawl. I feel guilty that I did not have a happier marriage so that my daughter's brief life could have been happier.

I have yet to meet a person who does not live with some sense of guilt for something he wishes he had done or not done. For most of us, our guilts are really regrets that we have not been all that we could have been.

The woman who was not there to hold her husband's hand at the time of his death says that she feels a deep guilt. Her guilt is really a regret that she had not been who she wished to be. She is saying,

"We went through so much together, for better and for worse. I wanted us to go through these last moments together, too." What makes this regret turn to guilt is perhaps that she can no longer repair that regret. Her husband is gone. There is no tomorrow in which to hold his hand.

We are left with what feels like a permanent loss, for now we can never create in our relationship the goodness, the fullness, the love that we long for. Our guilt springs from our truest self and expresses our deepest desires to be fully alive. It is as if there is some inner design to who we are, propelling us to become our full selves. As always, we can only hope to fulfill this design, to express it in our thoughts and deeds. As always, we can only try and will always fall short, for we are only human, we are only learning how to love. What matters is our intention, our deep desire to express the best of ourselves.

If your guilt becomes severe, it can cripple, it can stifle hope, and without hope life cannot unfold. When there is a good reason for us to feel guilt because we have intended to harm someone, it is even more important that we forgive ourselves. Unrelenting guilt and self-punishment do not serve life. It is important that we allow our guilt to soften with self-forgiveness into a sense of true remorse. These softer feelings are very painful, for they contain true sorrow for what cannot be repaired. We can move through this sorrow by accepting it and allowing it to move through us. But self-punishment is immovable. In it we become stuck and unable to express who we really are. This in turn produces the guilt of feeling that we are not being our true selves.

The way we can best live with our regret for being less than we wanted to be toward a loved one who is gone is to turn toward life more fully and openly. In this way, we put down seeds of new beginnings, of new hope, of new life. The man who feels guilty that he could not love his mother can go on to show his love to others. I cannot go back to remake a failed marriage, but I can bring that desire for wholeness to other relationships. In this way, life goes on, growth continues like a strand weaving through all of our relationships. In this way, hope continues.

During this week, allow yourself to contemplate what it was that was not fully lived with the person you are grieving for. What aspect of yourself do you long to carry forth, to give expression to in your life? Plant this as a seed that will grow slowly out of the darkness of your grief.

Anger is a
natural grief feeling.

Simon has a twin brother, Carl, who is dying of AIDS. He has been in and out of hospitals for the past two years. Simon has been grieving for some time, and a large part of his grief has been anger. To lose a twin is to know the depth of the paradoxical truth that we are at the same time part of one another and alone. We are all one, part of one life, one spirit, one earth, and one universe. Yet we are alone, we are born alone, we die alone. Simon and Carl were born of one egg, experienced a special kind of oneness. So they also feel more acutely the cut of the separateness that death brings.

Simon tells me that he cannot bring himself to walk in the park this spring. He cannot bear to see the beauty of life blooming. He finds himself raging at life. How can life be returning in all of its radiance when his brother is dying? He cannot understand this, he cannot bear it. His face is dark, he is in a storm. His eyes are on fire. I ask him to close his eyes, to see what his rage wants to do. He sees himself beating his fists on a wall. His fists are beating on the Wailing Wall. The wails of his rage are wrapped up in his anger. He beats his fists and wails. Simon is sobbing. His anger, his rage, once felt, once expressed, opens to the heart of grief, to the well of his tears, to his heartbreak.

Anger is a natural feeling when we are grieving. We are at a profound loss. Our love is powerless. We can do nothing as we stand at this loss. We can bring nothing back. We stand in empty time, in empty space, feeling small in this vast universe that gives and takes. In our helpless shock, we are appalled. How can this happen to our loved one? To us? How could Simon be left and his brother taken away? Simon wants to know, Why couldn't it have been me? It all feels like a game of dice, he says. It is all so random. Simon screams that he wishes he believed in God, so that he could hate him, rage at him. And for those who believe? It seems to me that God would understand Simon's anger at Him, for it is the other side of his love, an expression of the depth of his loss and of his bewilderment, of his "why?"

Anger at the loss of someone we love needs to be felt, needs to be expressed. It is a very powerful force that is moving through us.

When Linda's son died of leukemia, she became very quiet. She went dead in her shocked grief. She could not cry. Her grieving anger froze her. One day, in the early fall, she was walking on the beach. She was alone, the beach was empty. The waves were loud and their sound surrounded her. She felt safe. She began to cry. She continued to walk slowly along the beach, weeping softly. She walked for a long time. Slowly, her tears gave way to screams. The sound of the waves muffled her screams. She could scream as loud as she needed to. Her screams pierced her frozenness. They tried to pierce the invisible curtain that separated her from her son. Her screams tried to pierce the curtain between life and death. Then she lay down on the sand and wept and wept. The waves softened. They soothed her. Slowly, she came back to life. Her screams helped to deliver her back. They broke the prison her frozen pain had been building.

We need to soften our anger so that it does not imprison us. The only way to soften it is to accept it, to feel it, to know it as natural to us. We may feel anger toward our loved one who has died. Or anger toward ourselves. Or anger toward life, toward God, toward death. Once allowed, once given space, our anger softens into grief. Grief flows through us, grief hurts terribly. Grief is a part of our aliveness. Aliveness can hurt terribly. Sometimes we are afraid of it, to feel the aliveness of our grief, so we hold on to anger. We hold it tight and it turns gray, it turns to ashes, deadens us into bitterness. Bitterness is grief anger gone hard, hardening us. This is an anger to be feared because it deadens us, keeps us from life, depresses us, keeps us from going on.

Kate remained bitter for ten years after her husband died. She then came to therapy because her life was stuck. She had never formed a new relationship, never felt fulfilled with her work. She knew something was wrong. I gave Kate a pile of pillows and asked her to pound on them. As she pounded, she gradually got in touch with the source of her anger beneath her bitter, depressed exterior. She reached the grief that had been frozen within her for ten years. She screamed for her loss. She cried for the first time in ten years. She felt alive. She had returned to life.

This week, allow yourself to know that your anger is part of your grief. Let yourself feel it. Let yourself listen to it. Your anger has words. If it has no words, it has a sound. Hear it. Let it tell you what it needs, what it wants to do. Try to find the way and the place for you to feel your anger. Do you need to find a place to scream? Do you need to put the words of your rage somewhere? With a friend? A clergy person? A bereavement counselor? In your journal? You can draw your anger, finding the colors of it, the movement of it. Do you need to release your anger physically? You can take the pillows in your bed and pound them with your fists. There are many ways to release the anger of your grief. During this week, know which is your way and allow it to be.

Sometimes I feel
like a lost child.

Simon's brother has died. Carl has finally succumbed to the long, eroding ordeal of AIDS. On the night Carl died, Simon had taken him to the emergency room. The emergency room was very busy, and the staff instructed Simon to wait outside until the doctor arrived. Simon screamed, "I can't leave him! You can't separate me from my brother!" Over and over he screamed, crying in the waiting room, until the doctor called him and told him that Carl would probably not survive the night.

Simon held his brother's hand through the night. Carl died as the sun began to come up. Simon left the hospital just as the light of day was breaking. He did not know how he could be leaving his brother alone, forever. He kept walking through the streets, like a stranger in an unfamiliar place, numb. He felt lost, wanted to turn around, go back to the hospital, back to his brother. Simon kept walking, dazed and bewildered.

He walked, not quite knowing how he was walking, or where. He just walked, like a sleepwalker. He found himself in the park. He continued to walk for a long time. Everything and everyone seemed very far away from him, not quite real. Parents taking their children to school, dogs being walked, people jogging and cycling. The world moved before him as if in a dream.

Simon recalled how, as a child, he had been in a large department store with his mother and brother. When he looked toward them, they were no longer there. Somehow, Simon had gotten separated from them. He could recall feeling stricken with terror, small in a huge and suddenly strange world. No brother's hand to hold. Just as he now felt walking in the park. He walked and wept. There was nothing else to do. No hand would find him. He was at a loss, and lost.

At some point, Simon came to a lake. It was very quiet there. He sat down at the lake's edge and stared out at the water for a long time. He stared up at the heavens. The lake went on and on and around a bend out of sight. The heavens went on beyond the horizon. Through the veil of dazed grief, Simon's gaze rested on the water, on the endless rippling. It seemed as if one wave were moving endlessly, never ceasing, just flowing on and on. Simon sat there for a very long time. Something about the movement of the water, the ceaseless flow of the one wave, soothed his sense of lostness. He came back to this spot every day, all through the summer. It became his spot of solace, as he just sat gazing out over the waters and up at the endless clear blue sky.

One day, as Simon sat there, listening and watching the ripples on the water, he could almost sense the water speaking to him, saying, "The flow of life never stops. There is only one wave, flowing on and on. You can't see the water rippling beyond the turn of the bend. You can't see the sky beyond the horizon. You can't see your brother beyond where you left him. But they all go on and on."

Simon could sense, as he sat there, that something of his brother went on and on. Just as the wave, the heavens, and the silence did. As the silence around him. As the light and the breeze came through the tops of the trees. Simon ached with grief, but he did not feel like a lost child anymore. In this moment, he could feel Carl around him. In the silence, in the light, in the endless wave. He understood in this glimmering moment that death is somehow not an ending, nor is birth a beginning. He did not really understand more than this glimmer of something going on and on. As he bent his head, Simon could see that all around were forget-me-nots, fragile and tender, like his tears, like life itself.

During this week, give yourself time to meet the child in you who may be feeling lost in grief. Take the time to sit quietly, with closed eyes and easy breathing. Take this child to a lovely, calm, quiet lake. Sit there together. Let the child speak to you. Let it cry if it needs to. The more this child can have space, the less lost it will feel. So give it time and just sit with it by the lake. See the water just flowing by you. As you hear the sound of the water, listen to what it says to you, listen to what it says to the child who feels lost. You may wish to write of your experience in your journal. You may wish to let the lost child within you write in your journal for a few minutes each day this week. As this child is able to find the words for its lostness, it will find its way—the hand of life itself will guide it.

I let the pain
move through me.

Let yourself imagine that you see a stream. See how it flows naturally, as the water carries the life of the stream along. Now let yourself see a stream that has become dammed up, blocked. See how it cannot move, cannot flow. See how it accumulates heavy rocks, debris, living things that get caught, that cause further blockage to the natural movement of the life of the stream.

We are like the stream. Our feelings are meant to flow, to stream through us. Look at any contented animal, at any contented child. You can see how their feelings—love, sorrow, anger, desire—flow through them. You can see this in their bodies. Crying, rage, happiness, move through a soft, open body. Their muscles may tense in a moment of fear or anger, and then that momentary tightening loosens into tears, screams, laughter.

But something happens to most of us along the way. We become blocked just like the stream. Most of the time, we do not even know we are cut off from the flow of our feelings. "Don't cry, don't be afraid, don't be needy, don't be angry, be a big girl, a good girl, a big, brave boy." These messages are heard by our muscles, by our deep organs, by our hearts, and so we become like that blocked stream, damming up our feelings, particularly our intense feelings like grief, anger, love, loss, need.

Anytime we cut off our feelings, we tighten. Tightening against sorrow, pain, crying makes our feelings and body harden. See for yourself. Tighten your arm, your leg, your stomach, your brow. Hold it. Sense how hard you become just where you tighten. This is the same for your deep feelings, too. Hard pain cannot move, cannot flow, is blocked and buried and keeps our lives from moving on.

Molly's son died. She cried for a while and then threw herself into her work. She worked day and night, and for a while cried herself to sleep every night. Then she stopped crying. Soon afterward, she developed a severe sinus condition for the first time in her life. Her sinuses had to be drained every month. One of her doctors knew of her loss, and he gently suggested to her that her sinus trouble could be a result of blocked-up tears. His suggestion helped her to tell her tears that it was okay for them to move. She did this daily, unblocking the accumulation of sorrow that she had dammed up. Molly began to cry again, to allow her pain to soften, her tears to flow. Her sinus condition soon cleared up and her trips to the doctor stopped.

Molly found out that her tears did not go on forever, nor did they stop her from working. These two fears had made her stop up her tears. Softly she let them flow for her son, for her husband, and for herself, and they softened her heart.

During this week, give yourself some time, somewhere between twenty and thirty minutes. Plan not to answer the telephone. Find a relaxing position, either sitting in a comfortable chair or lying down. Loosen anything tight. Just let yourself be still. Listen to the sounds around you. The sound of the clock, the bird outside the window, the radiator, the soft music in the background. Listen to your own breathing, the rising and falling of it.

Now let yourself feel any tight places in your body. Just as you looked at the stream to see how it was blocked, look into your body the same way. Your chest, your back, your stomach, your heart, your jaw. Take your time. If you find an area of tightness, don't try to change it. Let it be. Just be with it. Place your hand on it. Let yourself ask, What am I tight against? What don't I want to feel? Let the tightness itself answer you. Maybe you are holding back tears, loneliness, feelings of missing the one who has gone—maybe you are afraid of the emptiness. Let the feelings come, let them speak to you.

You may feel a softening. You may continue to feel a tightness that cannot soften, cannot move. That is okay. Let it be. Accept it. This time of being with yourself in this way is just what you need. To hear yourself so that you are not lost to yourself. Slowly, very slowly, spending time like this each day will bring a melting, a sense of healing.

You may want to keep your journal beside you and write down your feelings. If you have a vivid picture of what is tight within you, of what turns to flowing or does not, you may wish to use colored pencils and draw what you have seen. You may ask the area in your body that is closed, what it needs. It may say, "I need to be touched, I need to cry, I need to scream, I need . . ." Ask in yourself and you will hear. If you hear with acceptance and compassion, the feeling of pain within you will gradually loosen and you will find that wrapped within it is its own solace.

Sometimes I feel depressed and need to move through my grief physically.

Often when we feel prolonged pain, as in grief, we feel like Dorothy, who said during a depressed period of her grieving, "I don't know what's wrong with me. All I want to do is sleep. I can't think of doing anything else." She wondered if she was ill, but a medical examination showed that nothing was wrong with her. It was clear to her family and friends, however, that since her husband's death six months earlier, Dorothy walked as if she were tired, talked in a heavy way, and felt a lack of desire to participate in her everyday activities.

Our tears, sorrow, anger, regrets may have become so intense during our grief that they have become congealed and stagnant within our body, resulting in our feeling depressed, slowed down, unmoving. There is a line that we move across during grief: on one side of the line our feelings are flowing, and on the other side we need to be quiet and still in the midst of loss. It is when this stillness becomes chronic that we are in danger of becoming depressed. Depression is grief that has stopped moving.

When we become depressed in this way during bereavement, it can be very helpful to visit with a counselor or join a group of other people who are mourning the loss of a loved one. Sharing feelings and experiences with others who are going through loss can be a source of solace and support and a help to keep our feelings moving.

It can also be of help if during this period a person can do what he or she may least want to do, and that is to move. You may have to give yourself a push. You may ask a friend to meet you and spend some time with you each day to do some physical activity. The company of a friend may help to get you started. The energy of a friend may help to charge your energy. To walk, to run, to work in the garden, to swim, to clean the house. These activities require no mental effort at all. They are rote. They are just movement. Our heart does not need to be there. Nor does our mind need to be there. Just our body moving.

What happens when we become depressed is that our energy stops moving through us. In physical movement, the stream of energy is opened.

When my friend Jim was grieving the loss of his brother, he asked me to go for a walk with him during a time when he was trying very hard not to fall through the crack into depression. There was a lovely reservoir in our neighborhood, where Jim often went to run. But on this day he could barely muster the energy to take a brisk walk. And so we walked slowly, at first without talking much. As we walked on for a while, he began to talk, not about anything very important, just to make contact. I could sense how his energy lifted as we continued our walk and talk. His voice sounded more alive. His face had more color than I had seen in it for quite a while. He even laughed at a certain point on the road when we saw some young squirrels chasing each other.

It was clear to me, in watching what happened for Jim as we walked, that the physical exercise of this not very energetic walk had a strong effect upon his mood. As we get more oxygen into our system, we are more invigorated, and as we become more invigorated, we feel more alive. That is why even modest physical activity can be a good medicine for depression. And as we move, we are affirming that we are willing and wanting to enter the flow of life again—that we are, in fact, alive and moving rather than deadened in our depression.

During this week make some time for yourself to do some physical activity. Without pushing yourself too hard, let yourself approach some kind of movement in a soft and easy way, even if your movement is not vigorous. Be aware of your breathing. If you do not find it possible to get yourself moving very much, you can still be in touch with your breathing as you sit in your chair. Just feel yourself breathing in through your nose and out through your mouth. As you breathe in, see yourself receiving life, and as you exhale, let yourself sense yourself giving to life. As you breathe out, see yourself letting go of any heavy and stuck energy within you. As you breathe in, see yourself taking in the energy of life, radiant and fresh.

You can do this breathing exercise as you take a walk or swim or run. Whatever movement you are doing this week, let it be with an awareness of your breathing and of your releasing any blocks in the stream of your energy. Sense yourself as a stream, unblocking, receiving fresh light and flowing in the current of life.

The only way through grief is to face it.

As the door of our grief opens, we are led from one thing to another, for the door of grief leads to a journey. This journey has its own map and its own timetable. Although each person must move through grief in his own unique way, there are places we experience that are common to us all.

We each experience the shock of suddenly being at a loss. Even if someone has been dying for a protracted time, their death is still sudden, still received with a sense of shock. We all live through long and empty nights. We all know the sense of feeling like a lost child. We all know numbness and bewilderment. We all know the feeling of searching for a loved one—on a street, in dreams—not able to accept the finality of loss. We all know how long is the pain of reconciling ourselves to finality. We all know the bafflement of going on while not knowing how to go on.

If we allow ourselves to keep the door of grief open, if we allow ourselves to stay open, to go through the facets of our grief, if we gently allow ourselves to close and open, to open and close this door that is our heart, the journey takes us somewhere that we could not otherwise have known. To be cut off from life, as we are only when we face death, to be thrown into an aloneness that can only be felt so utterly in grief, brings something unexpected to us. It is only when the kernels of our sorrow fall to pieces in the depths of our own darkness that some grain may grow from it.

While living through aloneness, which is at first excruciating, I slowly discovered the meaning of solitude. As I went through the long nights alone, as I sat by the lake, as I looked up at the empty sky, as I walked aimlessly through the park or the streets, I experienced the depth of an aloneness I had never known before. The pain I felt was the pain of having been ripped by death. As I went through this pain, as I lived with it, I began to feel moments of silence. If I sat through the silence, sometimes a sense of depression came over me. But at other moments that silence within me went on being just a silence. It was a peacefulness.

It is in this peaceful silence that arises in us unexpectedly that we come to know the solace of solitude. At first, we are aware only of glimmering moments that appear as a respite from unrelenting grief, as when we notice for the first time that a physical pain has stopped hurting. Only this stopping appears from somewhere deep inside of us as a sense of tender quietness. It arises out of the pain of our aloneness. From out of our solitude, we discover a capacity to be alone that we never knew before.

In this solitude, we can come to know better who we are. We develop an inner space in which to come home to ourselves. We can rest in this solitude, hear our inner voice, our feelings. We can carry our grief into our solitude and give it a place to rest, a place that within time becomes larger than grief itself and can hold it. Out of our own solitude, we gradually discover the solitude that is at the heart of all things, their center of light and silence.

Simon walks alone in the park, sits by the lake, looks at the heavens. He sits here often, and slowly he discovers a way of healing. As he walks in the park, he notices the light falling on a leaf. He stops. He is touched by the essence, by the solitude, of this leaf. In the same way, as he walks, he is touched by a child's face, a dog's eyes, an old person's slow step. Over the weeks, the months, over the years, his aloneness becomes a deep sense of solitude at the center of his heart where he is touched by life. Somehow, out of the anguishing aloneness brought by death, arises the solitude that is touched by the sacredness of life.

During this week, give yourself time to be quiet. Find a quiet, comforting place to sit. Close your eyes. If you wish, play some quiet music, or just listen to the sounds of the silence. As you become quiet, feel your breath. As you breathe in through your nose, sense how you are receiving life. And as you breathe out through your mouth, sense how you give to life. As you breathe in this way, let your breath guide you to a quiet space within your body. Put your hand on this place. It may be in your heart, your solar plexus, your stomach, or some other place within you that you find your place of quiet. Now just keep your hand there and continue to breathe.

See yourself breathing in a beautiful, clear, and radiant light. See the color of this light, let it fill this quiet place within you. See the space become larger and see yourself sitting within it. Are you at a lake, or a mountain, in a garden, at the sea? See where you are. Know this as your place of solitude. Be here. Be still. Breathe quietly. Hear the silence within you. Bring any sadness, any sorrow, any tears here. Let it be held in this silence, in your solitude. This place is always within you. Come here for a few minutes each day so that you can foster your solitude.

Little things
may trigger my grief
unexpectedly.

☐

Several months after Sally's husband died, she was walking along the avenue with a friend. It was one of those times that, without even realizing it, she was not thinking of Fred. Then her husband's barber passed and said a warm hello. Sally's tears welled up. The wound of her grief opened.

When we lose someone, there are echoes of that person all around us. At home, in the local stores, out at dinner. At the turn of some corner, we are surprised by grief.

A while after Ken lost his wife, he was ready to accept the invitation of a friend to go to the movies. Sitting there, he saw a man put his arm around a woman. This opened the ache of loss in his heart. He cried off and on during the film. His friend reached over and touched his shoulder.

There is no hiding from our grief. If it is fresh, it will keep aching with the pain of an open wound. Most of our friends and family will try to help us close the opening. We often try ourselves to tighten our muscles, wipe our eyes, push the tears down, go on walking down the street, go on talking, afraid that if we stay open, we will never be able to go on. We have already talked about how this kind of tightening against the opening of our feelings only stores the grief in tightened parts of ourselves. Grief waits there, sometimes for many years, sometimes for a lifetime, to open.

It is not easy to stay open when our grief is unexpectedly opened. It helps if we have a friend like Sally's or Ken's who can touch a shoulder or say, "Don't worry, it's okay, just cry, just let it go through you. There's no need to talk right now." But whether or not we have friends and family around us who can accept the movement of our grief, we can give this acceptance to ourselves.

During this week, when you are surprised by something that opens your grief, let yourself become aware of any way in which you tighten the muscles in your body as if to say, "Pull yourself together." Then let yourself breathe, let go, let the tears come. If you are with someone, at dinner, in a store, driving, reassure that person that you are "just crying, it's all right." People who think they need to reassure us, to help us pull together, need to be reassured by us.

This week, let yourself know that you are going to be fine if you let your grief go through you. At home, in your privacy, you may let small unexpected events that happened during the day open again so that your feelings can flow through you freely and fully. This is the only way with grief, to face it when it comes, to let yourself be open, to let it go through you so that you can go through it and go on.

In grieving,
it is also myself
that I mourn for.

When someone very close to us dies, we lose a part of ourselves with them. Parts of us die. When we grieve, we grieve for the one who is gone and also for ourselves. We feel dead because a part of us is dead. For many of us, what dies is the part of ourselves we have most strongly identified with. Wife, husband, father, mother, friend, lover, daughter, son. "Who are you?" "I am a mother" or "I am a wife" or "I am a..." When this identity dies, a person's sense of self can be shattered. It feels as if there is nothing and no one to go on with. We feel that we have lost the other and ourselves. It feels as though the ground has been taken from under our feet.

My dear sister-friend Nina died just before my fiftieth birthday. I was losing a friend I had known since I was twenty. She had been with me during all the important adult landmarks of my life. When I looked at her, she reflected to me all that was me, my history. She knew me as mother, daughter, wife, teacher, friend. As I approached my fiftieth birthday, I was letting go of many of those parts of myself that I thought of as me. I was letting go of my mothering self, as well as my youthful self. There was a sadness to letting go and a not-knowing who I would become as I grew older. When my friend Nina died, I realized how much our long-time friendship held our sense of mutual history, our sense of mutual identity.

This is what we lose when someone we have spent a long time with dies. If we try to hold on, it is even more painful. Some people hold on tight, afraid to let go, afraid that nothing more will be there. They may tell the old stories over and over again, or keep the house the same as it used to be. They may refuse to make new friends. They stop growing and are in danger of living a dead life by holding on too tightly to what must be let go of.

Only in letting go, only through mourning parts of ourselves, can we begin a new beginning and go on. Dying cracks us open. If we stay open, if we live through the dying, a new existence, a new hope can begin for us. For a while, we may not know who we are. We will feel like strangers on the earth, like a stranger to ourselves. We may need to wait for a time in this place of being at a loss. Seeds of a new self are growing through this darkness. In our grief, we do not know this. Seeds take time to grow, to open. They need the darkness.

Someone once said that waiting for a new sense of being is like waiting a long time for a train to come. What do we do while waiting for the train? We read the newspaper; we talk to the person next to us, thankful that he is there; we stare into space; we write in our journal; we pray.

And just as we begin to think that the train will never come, it does. Through the dark tunnel, the light of something new breaks through.

This week, find the quiet time to ask yourself, What part of me is dying? What part of me am I letting go of? You may want to write in your journal. You can speak to yourself just as you spoke to the loved one who has died, saying good-bye. You can write your tears, your upset, your anger or sorrow. You can give comfort. You can plant the seeds of new beginnings, of a new self. If you sense a new self within you, greet it, ask it who it is, what it needs from you in order to grow. Give it your love.

Through grief
I discover tenderness.

☐

In the weeks before Ellen's husband died, he would turn to her and ask, "Will you be all right? Will you be okay if I die?" He was getting weaker by the day and knew he was dying. But Ellen could not tell him that she would be okay after he died. She felt it would be a lie. She really did not know if she could or even wanted to survive without her husband. Her only response to his question was "I don't know. I can't say. But don't worry about me." But he did worry about her. He chose to die in the presence of their son, while Ellen was at home, as if to spare her. His last words to his son were, "Help Mom pull through."

Ellen went through a very difficult time. Her son and his family offered the consolation of their love and presence. But Ellen could accept none of it. She did not turn her family away. She was not unkind. She was just not present in spirit. Her family and friends were concerned that she might become very

deeply depressed and they urged her to see a psychotherapist who dealt with grief.

That is how Ellen and I came to meet one another. We
sat together very quietly. She had no words. She had only
her emptiness and the shock of still being alive when her
husband wasn't. We sat over several months, Ellen crying
bewildered tears or just sitting there in the silence of the
room, talking very little. It was good for her to be able to
sit in this way, in the company of someone for whom she
did not have to talk until the words came. I waited with
her, listening to the silence, both of us waiting for the hope
that would enable her to go on.

Ellen stayed in that nothingness for some time. She did
not push it away. She cried in it. She was there with her
grief in an open way. Both of us knew that grief was not
something to be gotten over the way an illness is. If we
stay with true feelings, even the feeling of no-feeling, even
the sense of I-am-nothing, something moves through us,
something rises out of our darkness.

Out of Ellen was born a tenderness that she never had
known before, that she could not have known before the
loss of her husband, for this tenderness comes only out of
knowing how precious life is through losing it. Ellen's tenderness ran very deep within her. It seemed connected to
the source of her being, just as her grief had been.

Ellen did survive. She survived with a tenderness toward her own frailty, her weakness, toward some part of
her that was broken and could be mended only with tenderness. She spoke of a tenderness toward all of life. She
found herself less angry, less irritable. She told me how on
the train an old man with a cane had been offered a seat by
several people. She said that she had wept to see how people were tender toward one another. She was touched by

small things that rise out of the heart as she had never been before.

After several months, Ellen went away on a trip to New England by herself. She wrote to me:

> It's very quiet here. The birds sound quiet. The trees bend this way and that. The wind moves through the trees. The quiet poppies are gleaming. The sun is streaming down like sweet honey. My heart feels full of life, of a tender love for all that surrounds me. It all speaks of shining hope.
>
> I give my tears to this shining tenderness in my heart. I am part of the field, part of this shining world. I am one of the flowers in this meadow. The sun shines on me too. Tears of sorrow still well up in me. And I turn as if to a lover and place all this into the arms, onto the breast of the light that is all around me.

Ellen describes the tender life that has poured itself into her grief. This solace cannot be made to happen. It cannot be forced. It can only take form out of our aloneness, like a light that comes out of darkness. During this week, reach for your own tenderness. Treat yourself tenderly. Hold your tears in your tenderness, your anger, your sorrow. Be as tender to yourself as you would be to someone dear to you who would be grieving. Know how precious your life is. Be tender toward it.

My dreams
can show me
the way.

Someone once said, "A dream not looked at is like a letter from God that is left unopened." Our dreams carry messages for us that we might not otherwise receive. They bring parts of us to ourselves that are deeper and often wiser than our waking awareness. Our dreams come from an inner source that contains things we don't know with our waking minds. So it is important that we give our attention to our dreams.

Dreams can help us face reality more deeply than we are able to do in waking life.

Charlotte dreamed of her husband: "Bill is out on the porch. I call the doctor to say that he's out there. I tell the doctor to come to see him, maybe he's alive. The doctor tells me that he'll come but that I should not go out there. The message I get, even though he doesn't say so, is that he knows that Bill is not alive."

It can take many dreams like Charlotte's to help us accept the stark reality of our loss. Even years later, a dream like this one might appear, coming from our deep unconscious, where relationships are eternal. In this way, dreams are to us what play is to children. If you watch, you can see a child playing the same game over and over until he makes sense of what is difficult for him in reality. And so we should not be surprised if our mind tries to make sense of our reality by having the same or similar dreams over and over again.

In dreams we can redo things in a way that we could not at the time of death. Yesterday, on the grass, I saw a dead bird. Its head was poised sideways, turned as if toward some surprise, as if in the moment of death it was bewildered. Its look was very innocent and fragile. I picked it up, carried it over to an herb garden, and placed it in a corner on the rich soil. I felt that I was bringing it to a home where it could be at peace and give its nourishment to the earth. That night, I dreamed:

I am walking in the street with my father. He is ill and says that he does not want to die in the hospital. I take him home, where he is dying in bed, with all those close to him surrounding him. He has the same look on his face as the bird. His eyes are looking up to death with innocent surprise, questioning what is beyond his comprehension.

In this dream my father is dying as I would have truly wanted him to, surrounded by the tenderness of love. Caring for the bird and its resting place tapped my deep unconscious desire that my father could have died at home. In the dream it could still have happened. There, that wish could be fulfilled.

In our dreams, we sometimes feel that we are visited by those we love and have lost.

Isaac is often visited by his beloved grandfather when there are important life decisions he needs to make. It is as if his grandfather comes to him carrying the wisdom he needs at these times.

As Charlotte was getting ready to cross the bridge from the past to a new future, she dreamed that her husband, Bill, came to her, opened her hand, and placed a seed upon it. He put one finger over his lips to indicate that there was no need to speak, and closing her hand over the seed, he disappeared. Charlotte received this message clearly, that Bill wanted her to go on, holding the seed of new beginnings.

During this week, give your attention to your dreams. Keep your journal next to your bed when you go to sleep. You can open your journal to a blank page, take your pen, and write in the middle of the page, "Please bring me a dream," encircling this request to your dream world in a golden circle, just before you close your eyes to go to sleep. When you awake, stay still for a while, giving yourself the time to recall your dream, letting it wash ashore into your morning consciousness. Then write it in your journal. After you write your dream, close your eyes and listen for what the dream may be trying to tell you. Let yourself be open to its message and try to sense if it is giving you some guidance that you can follow.

I choose
my personal ritual
of remembrance.

It is a year since Bob's wife died. He and his family gather together to plant an area of the garden as a memorial. They spend the day turning the earth, enriching it, planting the rosebushes that Dorothy would have loved. This is a place they can return to each year at this time, a place to share their love for Dorothy and to give expression to it in an alive way.

A memorial observance brings together those who best knew and loved the one who is gone. By sharing in the creation of the observance, they keep alive the spirit of the person and honor that person's essence. Even if people cannot gather, they know that something has been done to remember and to give love.

Diane and Arthur married long after his father died. Each year, on the anniversary of his father's death, he would light a memorial candle. He would tell Diane of his father, share his memories and his sadness. Diane felt that she had come to appreciate this person who was so significant to her husband. One year, she was traveling without Arthur at the time of his father's memorial anniversary. She lighted a candle and told the friends she was with about her father-in-law, whom she never knew. She began to carry on her husband's love for his father.

Each one of us can find a ritual that becomes a meaningful way to remember a loved one we have lost. Each time we return to this ritual, it helps to open our heart and to honor the very best of that person with the very best of ourselves.

There is a basic wisdom to marking the time of a death after one year has passed. In some traditions such an observance is provided by a person's religion. In the Jewish faith, for example, a bereaved person stands up in synagogue every Sabbath when the mourner's prayer is said. After the first year of bereavement has passed, the person stands only once a year when the prayer is said.

During the year following my father's death, I observed this practice of rising for the mourner's prayer. I found it to be immensely healing. To stand each week with others who were mourning a loved one gave me the feeling of not being alone, of sharing an unspoken bond with people I did not even know but whose hearts I could feel holding an ache like my own. To know that I was not alone, to visibly and physically know myself as part of the human condition, made a profound difference to me. To stop standing at the first anniversary of my father's death was a definite marker—an aspect of grief was over.

That very act of not standing up anymore shifted the ground of my grief amid the community of grievers. Now others would take their turn to stand weekly. And so the wheel of life and death turned before my eyes.

We are all mourners and we are all comforters, to witness for those whose turn it is to stand and be counted in loss. To know that we are not alone, to know that we are part of the human condition is a great solace. For me it has made a profound difference. When my daughter died, I went through mourning in a very private way. Certainly there were loved ones around me, but there was little ritual. If I had been able to avail myself of the opportunity of solace that my tradition offered, I do believe that my grief would have been more bearable.

Our rituals help us to mark our circles on the ground of grief. But these rituals do not have to belong to any religious form. Our rituals can be very personal. We may not even like to use the word "ritual." Whatever it is that we find within ourselves to mark beginnings of grief, to mark a first anniversary, to mark future observances of a beloved's death, is what matters. Each year on the anniversary of my dog's death, I plant flowers at the apple tree under which he is buried. For my friend Nina, I light a beautiful candle next to some flowers that I put in a vase she gave me. It is a quiet evening, in which I give myself a space of solitude to remember, to miss, and to love. I may have friends to dinner, friends who never knew Nina, but the candle is there in the midst of the new to recall the old.

During this week, let yourself reflect on what observance, what ritual, would be most meaningful to you to express your love and memory of the person in your life who has died. You may wish to visit your synagogue or church to experience their practice for mourners. You may want to see if it is one that touches you, that belongs to you. If not, find for yourself your own simple way of remembering, particularly to mark the first anniversary of death.

Life
calls to me
tenderly.

□

Life will call again. Unexpectedly it will swell into the numbness, into grief, like an underground stream surging its way through the darkness. Life will call again quietly, like a surprise. Perhaps in the summer, when a sudden rain touches your body and it tingles with aliveness. Or in the spring, as you pass a budding tree. Or in the winter's first snowfall, as you are surprised by your childhood delight rising up from somewhere inside that you thought dead.

You may try to hold on to the deadness of your grief, afraid that your aliveness will take you even further from the one you want to hold on to. I remember that a few months after my daughter died, her little friend Sari said, "I used to be able to hear Leslie's voice, but I can't hear it anymore. It's gone far, far away." It's like that. Inevitably the voice grows pale and a curtain falls upon the past. It must be this way if we are to let life call us again, if we are to listen, to follow, as Sally did:

For the first time today, I saw the flowers. I heard them calling. I filled the vase with little yellow flowers and red buds from the garden and put them on the window over the sink in the kitchen where the sun lit them. I could feel some of their aliveness move in me.

As we allow life to move in us again, we are moved slowly toward life. We may invite a friend or two to dinner and find that we enjoy the shopping, the cooking, setting the table. We may find that we do these things more caringly, not taking them for granted. The lettuce may glisten more, the tomato be more red. As we return from a grief where all the colors of life have been drained, the colors of life seem more alive than ever before. We are called by life to a new beginning, a new hope, and a new reverence for life.

It is not easy to come through this ending of grief. We sat long in our grief. And there are parts of us that will go on mourning. Loss is pitched deep in the dark soil of our lives and is not an illness that is cured and gone. It becomes a part of who we are. But so is the light of life that is calling us a part of who we are. Sally spoke of this in her journal:

I look up at the skies. It is dawn. I see the morning star. It is neither day nor night. It is both end and beginning. I welcome the pale morning light of the sun into my heart. In the light I feel a blessing to go on. And I know too that my husband goes on in the same light. I bless the day and am comforted and grateful to be a part of life.

We are called by life to a new beginning, a new hope, and a new quality of reverence for life. Because we have known such darkness, the light of life calls us more deeply than ever before.

During this week, listen for the ways in which life calls to you. Write in your journal how you listened to life's call once during the day. Did you listen with a tear, with a smile, with both? Did you feel reluctant to follow this voice? Did you feel joyous? Whatever it is that you experience as you listen to the call of life, let it be, let yourself be touched.

Death
cannot
shatter love.

☐

Many months after Alex's wife died, he wrote to her in his journal. He said:

> Dear Natalie: We never unwound the hurts, the knots of anger, the resentments, the disappointments, the pent-up needs. They got all mixed up with our love. We never unwound them, at least not with words. But I did, during the last months, unwind them with my sense of love. As you grew weaker, I felt softer toward you, nearer to you, gentler. But never with words did we unravel things. Only with love.

Alex expresses for all of us the mixture of regret and love that are left by death. There is hardly a person who is left with a memory of a perfect relationship. We are human, and perfection is not our heritage. But as the months and years go by, the hurts and angers, the resentments and disappointments, the unlived hopes that remain from this relationship are there for us to work through. We work them through in the relationships that survive. In this way, we unravel the old knots. They dissolve into love. Love is what survives and all that matters.

Alex continued to write:

All that was remains a part of me, remembered and loved and held in my life. I hold so much that will become a foundation stone of a new life and I hold also that which is infinitely more than my past. It lights my life and my way. Love is all that is left, all that I need and all that I long for.

Love is all that is left. Love is the bridge that takes us forward. For many of us the path to that bridge lies in forgiveness, either of oneself or of the other. Forgiveness is what might be needed to do the unraveling that Alex speaks of. Forgiveness of himself for not having been softer sooner. Forgiveness of his wife for not having helped him or helped herself, for having died too soon for it to be possible.

During this week, ask yourself, What in my feelings do I need to unravel? What do I need to give forgiveness to? What blocks my love? Sit quietly for a while each day. Breathe into your heart. Close your eyes. See a light in your heart as you breathe into it. Is this the light of forgiveness? Is this a light of love? See the color of it. Look into your heart and let this light unravel what needs to be unraveled within you. Do this briefly each day.

On the last day of the week, let yourself find a flower that is the color of the light in your heart. Keep this flower where you can look at it, and remember, Love is all that is left. Love is all that I need and all that I long for.

What do life and death mean to me?

When you reflect on the word "death," what other words come to your mind? For most of us, "dark, terrible, frightening, alone, ghost" come to mind. The word "life" usually holds quite different associations. What are yours? Words like "whole, moving, growing, light, joy, together" usually come. These words call up images that are rooted deep within us and are very forceful in influencing the way we see things and think about them.

These words are only the tip of the iceberg of unconscious images within us—of our deepest understandings of reality. We can sometimes enter this unconscious realm through our imagination. There a door opens, and through it we can see wider horizons. In the guided journey that follows, you can explore what death and life mean to you beyond the surface images that you are aware of.

Isaac shared with me the fact that he was very afraid of dying. He was aware of a constant low level of anxiety that was connected somehow with this fear of death. It tightened him in life. When I asked Isaac what death meant to him, what his images of death were, he said:

"Death is being left alone. I remember my grandfather; he was the only person who loved me without any conditions: he just loved me simply and totally. I was only two when he died, but I can still see his face shining with love for me. And then suddenly he was gone. I lost him and his love, and in some terrible way I was alone. When I was five years old, I remember worrying a lot that my mother and father might die."

Isaac said that now, at forty, he was afraid to die —to be separated from himself, from his body, his wife, from everything he knew.

The fear of the separation that comes with death is familiar to all of us. We all know that terrible feeling of aloneness, of loss that Isaac felt when his grandfather died. These feelings cannot be erased. We can, however, look beyond these feelings toward other feelings, other knowings. Perhaps fear prevents us from looking, and when we do not look, we always fear the worst.

Isaac and I went on an imaginary journey to explore other images of death he was not yet in touch with. You can do the same, if you wish. It really does not matter whether you enter this journey before or after you read Isaac's experience, because your journey will be your own. Your imagination has a life of its own. It is best to do this with one or more of your friends so that you can share your experiences—and find together how you can come to a deeper sense of what death and life mean to you.

Relax. Sit in a comfortable chair, loosen any tight clothing, let yourself be guided:

See yourself growing old, having lived your life and now coming close to death. See where you are, how you look. Are you alone? Are others with you? Sense how you feel, in your body, in your spirit. See what happens as you pass from life to death. Take your time to experience all that is happening. Now see yourself having left your physical body. Watch your funeral service, see who is there, hear what people say about you.

From this new perspective, looking on from out of your body, look at your life and know what you would do if given the opportunity to go on with your life. How would you live a fuller life, be more the person you would have desired to be?

Now see the funeral ending and let yourself see what happens to this part of yourself that witnessed your funeral. What is this part of you? Who died? Who had a funeral? Let this part of you now return to your body that is sitting on the chair. Feel your back, your buttocks on the chair, touch your feet. Sense all that you feel and understand. Feel yourself fully alive. Are your images of death and life any different as a result of this journey? How would you have lived your life differently? How would you have lived a fuller life? Know that you can live this full- ness in your life now. Let yourself feel how, without the presence of death, life could not possibly be as precious. Our awareness of death gives life its fragile beauty.

Isaac's journey to meet death will help us to see how going beneath our fears widens our perspective and relieves our fear. Since we cannot possibly know the experience of death, because we have never experienced it, anything we feel or think about death is really about life. If we are afraid of death, we are tightening, now, against life. As Isaac lived through this journey, he gained something for himself that he could carry into his life to make it fuller.

I've lived longer than anyone I know. I'm in my nineties. I'm lonely. I don't play tennis anymore. I've read all I want to read. I've passed the point of fear. My fear of death is less strong than my curiosity. I don't see the point of fear anymore. My affairs are in order. I'm at peace. I'm ready to set forth. I'm aware of a certain energy coming into the room, a radiance. It's an ageless man. He beckons to me in a way that I have total choice. "Are you ready?" I nod.

I rise up and join him. I step out of my body. I look back at it. My eyes are closed. I'm looking down at my funeral. It's small, in a nice quiet country churchyard. I hear the talk about me. "He was a quiet and generous man. He was friendly and independent. He loved children and nature and animals." I feel touched by their love.

"I look at myself and I say, 'Isaac, you struggled too much, tried to control things too much. You could have relaxed more, been more open, trusted life more, smiled more, shown your love more.'"

Before he is buried, Isaac thanks his body for carrying this loving man. He feels that he has come to a deep peace with himself.

"My spirit rises. I see my father. He takes me through a big passageway, a tunnel that joins earth and heaven. At the top of the passage it's very bright and filled with calm, love, and compassion. I see all those people who've been important in my life: my wife, my grandfather, my mother, friends. I weep with happiness. I want to thank all those people for giving me so much. I have no regrets anymore."

When Isaac returned from this journey, he felt more than a release from his anxiety. He felt a great tenderness toward his life and toward those in it. He felt the presence of all who were gone, aware of the great continuity that lives through our love. He spoke of wanting to be in nature more, to smile more, of wanting to tell those close to him that he loved them.

Let yourself do the same. Let death help you to make life the fullest it can be. Let death help you be tender to your life, to all of life. This week, each day, before you start the busy day, ask yourself, What will make me most alive today, most fulfilled? And then be that aliveness, that fullness. Be life, and in so doing, you will give to life all of your fullness. This is the only way to meet life and to meet death, not only without fear but with the fullness of our whole being.

Out of this darkness,
my creativity
can be born.

Creativity does not mean writing the great novel. Creativity belongs to our inner impulse to give life, to give *to* life. Ellen, when she sat up during the long nights and found her way to put together a photo story of her life with her husband, was making a creative gesture toward her past and also toward the future lives of her grandchildren. To find our creativity is to hear within ourselves what our heart wants to express.

Some months after Jean's mother died, it was vacation time. She usually traveled, but this August she asked her husband if he would not mind spending vacation at home. Jean felt a very strong desire to do a massive cleaning of their house. She cleaned the drawers, closets, bookshelves. She threw things away that she had held onto for twenty years. She sifted through this and that, aware that as she sifted the wheat from the chaff she was clearing an open space for her future. Her mother had died. Her husband had just retired. She was at a crossroads in life. Some creative source within impelled her to do this cleaning, into which new life could enter.

There was one thing of the past that she was not ready to throw away. It was a gold paper crown that she had given her mother at her last birthday, the last time she had been hearty and happy. This was a memory Jean still needed a tangible sign of. What to keep, what to let go of, was a creative choice. This cleaning, this clearing, came from deep inside her and expressed her instinct to go on and create life with her husband.

Our journal can offer a place to express ourselves in a creative way. As we write, we can listen to ourselves in a deep way, hearing our inner voice speak without covering it with "woulds" or "shoulds." In this way, we hear what is within us, deep in the creative wellsprings of our life. In that place, we hold a clear sense of who we are, of what we long for, of the true direction of our lives. If we follow this voice, we cannot help but lead a creative life. Our inner voice may guide us to arrange a vase of flowers or a picnic lunch. The way we say hello to someone or look at someone and smile can be creative acts. They can all touch life and make a gesture of appreciation toward life.

If we listen to the wellsprings within us, as we go through grief and begin to touch life again, we may find ourselves moving toward a creative and new interest. As we feel more deeply aware of our appreciation for life, things that never called to us before may suddenly excite us.

After his brother died, Simon spent a lot of time in the park, at his spot by the lake. He began to take a keen interest in the birds that nested there. He would watch them for hours, intrigued by their habits and beauty. He got himself field glasses and for the first time in his life became an avid bird watcher.

Some years after her son died of leukemia, Linda began to volunteer one day a week to hold premature babies in the local hospital nursery. She helped these infants to be held into life. What could be more creative an act?

It was after my daughter died that I began to write in my journal to find words for my loss. I had never had any interest in writing before. It was writing in my journals during those years that led to my writing this little book.

Each of us, as we follow our own healing instincts, may be surprised to find that out of our search for solace, something of our creative self is born and finds expression. And out of this expression we are led back toward our love for life.

Find a comfortable place to sit. Close your eyes and focus your attention on your breathing. As you breathe, see yourself standing at a well of deep, clear, sparkling water. See a silver cup beside the well, tied to a long golden cord. Drop this cup deep into the water. Know that this is the well of life, of your life. Draw up the cup of water and drink it. As you drink this water, let it wash your heart. And now, with a clear, clean heart, listen to it tell you what it wants, what it needs, to express its love for life. Follow what your heart's voice tells you. Follow it with tenderness and with a wish to express the love of life that is within you. Let yourself know that with this love you bless life and in doing so you are expressing your creativity.

Go to the well of your life each day this week. Drink the water. Cleanse your heart. Listen to it and follow.

I learn to hear
the voice
of aloneness.

□

The voice of aloneness is one we must all learn to live with, for we are ultimately and basically alone. As we go through grief, we learn to live in our aloneness. We live through the long nights. We learn to be in an empty house, to be in our inner emptiness, to be with our tears, our ache, our sorrow, our memories. This is all part of what is woven into the fabric of our life, of who we are. If we try to run away from our aloneness, afraid of what we might find there, we can never be our real selves. In time, and with kindness to ourselves, we find an inner home for our aloneness.

For me, this space of aloneness is like the houses I have seen in Greece, painted all white, the walls inside white and bare, the sun entering through the doors and windows, the atmosphere very calm, very quiet, the silence of white. I sit in this space, a space I call alone, and I let the voice of my aloneness speak, weep, have its reveries, have whatever appears within these walls. A woman I know senses her inner place of aloneness as a warm, dark space, like a cave in a rich, quiet forest. It sits inside of her like my bare Greek room sits inside of me, always there for me to go to.

Grief has taught me not to be afraid of my aloneness but, rather, to be nourished by it. I never thought that would be possible during the early, long aching days and nights of grief. But slowly I began to make a circle around my alone time. Not necessarily to do anything special in it. I might have done the dishes, washed and dried the lettuce, listened to music, listened to the rain outside the window, taken a walk. I might have lain down and closed my eyes, not to sleep, just to enter the circle of my aloneness to find who I was there in that moment, what I really felt, what I really needed in those moments.

This space of aloneness, discovered in grief, has become a sacred space in which to find my true self and hear my true voice. During this time, I may write in my journal, finding through writing what I need to say to myself, or to someone else. Being alone is like being at the center of a circle, the center of myself, knowing always that the circle and the center are there to come to, an inner circle, an inner home.

Some people set a space for themselves within their home that becomes their space to come to aloneness in. It is best if the space is very simple, and it can be small. It should be in a part of the house where you can be alone without being disturbed by others.

During this week, create this space for yourself if you don't already have one. Make it a space that is comfortable, simple enough that you can feel it as your intimate place to come to. Come here for a while each day and let yourself be with your aloneness here, with anything that comes up in you. You may wish to keep your journal in this place so that you can have it near you to write in if you wish to.

While you spend your time in this outer space you have made for yourself, close your eyes, look within, and see what the inner space of your aloneness looks like. Make it as you need it to be. Know that it is always there within you to come to, to find yourself.

The mysteries of birth and death are entwined.

I want to paint a scene for you. You may already be familiar with it. If not, I would be surprised were you not to experience it sometime.

It is the beginning of spring. Perhaps it is April. You decide to go out for a walk in the early evening. Or perhaps it is morning. The air is balmy. Seemingly from out of nowhere, the grass is filled with crocuses and daffodils. The dogwood and cherry trees have begun to bloom. A fragrance fills the air. The birds are singing their songs through the treetops. It is all a wonder. Every one of your senses is newborn, awakened by the burst of life. You feel lighthearted. Your steps are buoyant.

Suddenly, you are aware of a strange, unexpected ache in your heart. It is an ache that you did not expect to feel at this moment. It is the ache of loss, an echo of your grief. Together, side by side, entwined, the thrill of new life and the ache of loss are there within you.

T. S. Eliot has called April the cruelest month. I think he meant that it is the most poignant, because it captures the mystery that our lives and all of life are wrapped in: the mysteries of birth and death. And because these two mysteries are so entwined—in all of nature, in the seasons, and in our hearts—I am able to paint this picture in which these two feelings course through us at the same time, when life is most vibrant and most awesome in its mystery.

In modern times, many of us are cut off from the cycles of birth and death. Those who still live close to nature, in the country, on the farm, are fortunate to see, daily, animals mating, being born, dying. They are used to seeing, year after year, the earth bearing fruit and multiplying and then lying fallow until new seed rises up from it. The Shakers used to make large cradles in which their elders rested by the fire just beside the smaller cradles that held the newborn. They dug their own graves with their own hands, made their own coffins, birthed their babies at home. In all of that, the perpetual turning of the wheel of death and birth and birth and death was part of a connected circle of existence.

In our movement away from nature, we have gained many benefits from life, but we have lost that rhythmic song of the turning wheel of life and death. For most of us, the intellectual knowledge of this wheel is present, but each birth and each death has become disconnected. Certainly, each birth and death is unique, for each soul, each life, is sacred. And yet it helps us if we stop to think about how we are a part of the ever-changing current of life. Each birth and each death can then help us to know how we are a part of the cosmic order of life, not cut off in the isolation of our loss.

I have a friend, a middle-aged woman, who has had the strange fortune of coming upon little birds who are wounded on city streets. Ever since she can remember, she has noticed this little bird with a broken wing, that little one with a broken leg, or she has been right in front of the tree when a bird fell from its nest, seen that little pigeon still alive but dumped in the garbage. She has not been able to pass them by and has taken many a bird home. She has given them good care, and some of them have eventually flown away, but most of them have died because they do not do very well in captivity.

The other day, my friend was walking up her street when she saw a small yellow bird that had fallen from a tree. It seemed quite well, but its leg was hurt, and after giving it some drops of water, hopeful that it would do well, she took it home. She put it on her back porch with some water and crumbs. She looked out at it and saw that it was sitting contentedly. Perhaps it could not fly because of its wounded leg. My friend gave me a phone call, and what she said will perhaps touch you as it did me:

"You know, it does not seem right for me to keep this little bird. It belongs to nature. Nature can take care of it better than I can. Nature knows how to take care of its living things. I would like to take it over to the park and set it by a tree. If it does not survive, then nature will still take care of it in its own way. Not everything in nature survives. But I feel guilty doing this even though my heart tells me to."

She went on talking and I said nothing, just listening to her as she went about making her decision. She said, "When I was younger, I could never have thought of doing this, of letting nature take care of a wounded bird. But since my father has died and my mother has become old, I have a different feeling. I am more accepting of the natural losses. I accept them as a part of life. Yes, I'll take the bird to the park. That is where it lives. Whether it lives or dies is not all that important. What matters is that it is in its home in nature."

When my friend returned to the porch, the little bird had already spread its wings and flown to where it had to go, once again part of the great natural cycle. But it had, in its short stay, taught my friend something of accepting the cycles of life and death, of how we are a part of some great natural cycle, the mystery of which we can only sense.

When I ponder this mystery, I think about the cycle of the year, of its four seasons, turning from birth to death to rebirth just like the seasons of our lives. Just like the seasons of our griefs.

This week, let yourself ponder this mystery. Whatever the season, be aware of it as part of a cycle, as part of a wheel turning. As you look at people, see their place in the cycle of life. And see yourself in this way as well. Call the loved one who has recently died to your mind and heart. See and sense this person as part of the ceaseless and mysterious process that all living things belong to. Know your feelings. They may be feelings of sadness, anger, poignancy, quietness, sorrow. Give these feelings words. Perhaps you will want to write whatever words you feel in your journal. Perhaps you will want to share them with a loved one.

I look at life
with a new
amazement.

After grief, we begin again. After a long journey through a dark night, we open the door and the light amazes us. After so long a darkness, the light comes to us as an amazing grace, as if from some divine source. As we are touched by life again, we sense a holiness at the heart of things. We look at a sunset, at a face, at a rain falling fresh and we hear an "Ah!" within ourselves. That "Ah!" is the sound of amazement made by a mind and heart that are seeing as if for the first time.

This seeing as if for the first time has been called a "beginner mind." It is a mind that sees the mystery of life in all things. It is a mystery how it happens that in loss our mind, our awareness, expands. We gain a sense of something beyond the limited time and space we are usually aware of. Something of the mystery of life, something of the light that always shines, something of the infinite touches us. In this amazement, we experience ourselves participating in the divine in our daily lives.

Our mind finds the sun in the smallest of things, and we

are amazed by grace in these moments of our lives. We do not need to go to the Grand Canyon to be amazed. We can walk down the street, drink a glass of water, sit under a tree, play with a pet or a child. Something of a quiet radiance shines through. We find that we do not need to possess or to evaluate things as we used to. It is enough to look, to appreciate, to touch the life we see with our eyes and heart.

When we have this sense of amazement, of the grandeur of life, it is not that we have abandoned our knowledge of how small we are in the face of death. Rather, it is precisely because we have come to know how small we are, because we have stayed in this feeling of smallness, that we are able to feel amazement at the infinite wonder of life, at the radiance that shines through.

Lauren spoke of her sense of amazement. She said, "This light that fills me, this light of the universe that I am, that is all things—it is my home. I live in this light. It is never not here. I take this light and spread it over me like a cape. I take this light and wrap it around the darkness. I offer myself to this light when I wake up. When I go to bed, I offer myself. I lift all things up to this light. I don't know why I wasn't aware of this beautiful light that is life before I knew grief, but I just didn't. Maybe, before, I just took life for granted, didn't know how golden it is."

During this week, set aside a moment in each hour to stop whatever you are doing. Look around you with a beginner's mind. Look at something, listen to something as if for the first time. A child playing, a person standing next to you at the bus stop, the grass growing. Whatever it is, let it be alive for you. Be amazed at the world.

The voice
of my loneliness
can guide me.

Loneliness and aloneness are not the same. In our aloneness, an inner space opens for us into which we can meet
who we truly are in this moment. We might encounter sorrow, tears, anger, memories. Whatever it is that we open to
in aloneness is our self, our realness. There is no one who
does not come up upon their aloneness if they are being
real.

Loneliness is different. Loneliness does not open us to
ourselves. It closes us down, it confines our living space.
Loneliness builds fences around our lives. Loneliness says,
"I don't have any friends. They were all my husband's
friends. There's no future for me. There's nothing I'm excited about. Life is boring. No one wants me. I'm lonely."

If we really listen to this voice of loneliness, we are able
to hear another voice wrapped inside it. It is a voice of
desire. If we drop deeper into listening to "I don't have any
friends, they were all his friends," we can hear the desire
of "I want friends of my own. I am lonely for friends of my
own. I long for that." If we listen to "There's no future for

me. There's nothing I'm excited about," we can hear "I want a future, my future. I want to be excited."

Our loneliness expresses what is missing for us. It holds our desire for life, our longing to go on, to be a part of life.

> Charlotte came to see me after her husband of many years had died. She was despondent because her life was stagnating. There were endless complaints about how lonely her life was, how work and her social life and her creativity refused to begin anew and hold some spark of life for her. As we met, Charlotte wept and gradually gave voice to her longing.

Giving voice to our longing can guide us in going on, in opening new doors to life. But going on also means saying good-bye to the past, and good-bye can be very painful. Some of us would rather hold on to our loneliness than express our longing and say our good-byes.

> Charlotte saw herself standing in the middle of a bridge, a bridge between the past and the future. She stood there in all her loneliness and longing and said good-bye to her husband. She told him that she wanted to listen to her heart's longing, to follow it. Then, crying, she turned and walked toward the future. Soon after, Charlotte joined an art class and began to paint for the first time in her life. There, she made new friends, her friends. Her loneliness lessened little by little, as she listened to the desires contained within it and let them guide her on.

Charlotte, like the rest of us, could only have a renewal of her life by allowing a letting-go.

This week, let yourself listen to your loneliness. Take two facing pages in your journal. On one side, let your loneliness have its voice, write what it says. And then, listen very quietly to hear what desire is wrapped within it. On the other side of the page, write this desire.

What does your desire want to guide you toward? Can you let yourself be guided? Do you need to stand on the bridge between the past and the future as Charlotte did? If so, stand there. Let the feelings and words of good-bye come up, the feelings of letting go that may block your following your heart's desire. Let yourself know if it is not yet time for you to have any desire. That is all right. The time must come from within you. You can always return to this mediation when you are ready to.

I sing a song even when it is a sad song.

It takes time for a song to be born. Not a forced song that you mimic because someone, sometime, said, "Don't cry, sing." Such a song is not a true song, one that is born out of the heart.

It was about a year after my daughter died that someone said to me, "It will take time. Time is the great healer." She said this to me because she had noticed that I still carried a pair of sunglasses in my purse. Not knowing at which unforeseen moment tears would well up within me—at work, at dinner, on the street—I came to rely on my sunglasses to provide me that dark privacy that tears need. "It will take time" was something I did not believe.

Today, from the distance of years, I can see that I did not want time to be a healer. I did not want time to separate me from my golden-haired child. My tears were a sign to me of my closeness to her. But I found that tears are not the only sign of closeness. I can still feel close to my daughter without tears. And time does indeed do its work of healing and turning our hearts toward the songs of life.

We journey through time. And as we journey through the time of grief, we are changed, just as we are changed by journeying through any land. The first country of grief we live in may be the land of tears that never seem to stop. They might well up out of a pain in your solar plexus or heart. This pain might feel like a cut. And, in fact, it is a cut, for the fabric of life you have woven with the one who is gone has been cut. He or she can no longer be seen, touched, or heard by you. In this land of tears, you may have no tears. You may ask yourself, Why am I not crying? No tears, no pain. Only numbness, a sense of deadness. If you sit in time, taking the moments to sit, to walk, with yourself, you may become aware that this very numbness is itself a crying, the crying of no-crying. As you accept this, no-crying may melt into tears. Time and self-acceptance are the keys that help, that melt, as you travel through grief.

Slowly, very slowly, you may find yourself in yet a new country in which tears have somehow moved toward silence. You may find that no matter what you are doing, there is a sense of silence that you carry within. It is a deep silence, and vast, and it holds a sense of mystery. When my daughter died, and I stood over her little body in its bed, there was a profound silence, my first sense of this silence. It is a silence that surrounds death. It came at the moment I felt my daughter's soul leave her body, an empty cocoon, upon the bed. This silence hovered while I said good-bye. When I left my daughter behind and walked out of the hospital into the spring rain, I fell into the desolate silence of tears, dark and despairing.

Through time, through tears, that first silence slowly crept back as if it had been waiting for the door of my heart to quiet and open. How can I describe this silence, neither dark nor despairing, this same silence that surrounded my daughter as she died? It is like the silence of a pine forest when the sun's rays shimmer through the trees, forming a cathedral of light and glistening green, or like the vast circles of silence that surround you far out at sea or on a mountaintop. If you have felt this silence find its way through your tears, let it. Don't be afraid of it. It is the awesome silence of the mystery of life and death. It is a silence beyond words. In it, you open your eyes wide, slowly you close them. You listen to know something of this mystery. Tears may well up, but they are no longer dark tears. As your eyes open wide to look somewhere out into the universe for an answer, or as they close to look within, you may find a light smile upon your lips. It is a smile that understands beyond words.

As you listen in this silence, you may feel your throat open. You may hear a song well up within you. This song may have no words. You may find your head moving up and down, the movement of "I understand," even though you have no words at all to put to that understanding. You may feel your mouth open, wanting to say something, to make a sound. "La, la, la, la-la, la," you may slowly sing over and over again, or "dee, dee, dee, dee," over and over and over again. For a long time. Maybe five or ten or fifteen minutes. Just letting the sound well up from within you. As you do this, first softly, then louder, then softly again, you may find yourself crying. This crying may carry your grief, a sadness from your deepest depths. Let it. It is a true song. This crying may carry an understanding that you have no words for. An understanding that this mystery of life and death is beyond our understanding.

You may sing in this way as you sit quietly, your hand holding your chin, or as you drive or wash the dishes. As you sing, you will come to yourself, to your true feelings, to your understanding. Life will come to you. Out of this silence a song is born. This song may find words as it sings through you. It is a song of sadness. It is a song of love. And ultimately, as we travel through time, it is a song of praise for the precious gift of life. I do not think we can find this song except through sorrow and by journeying through the country of grief. Once finding it, however, this capacity to find our song will never leave us, for it becomes a part of our nature to raise our sadness to song.

New loved ones
gradually
enter my life.

It is hard for us to imagine the door of our heart opening to let anyone new in after someone who has meant so much to us has gone. It is hard to imagine forming new and meaningful bonds with anyone else. People outside our immediate circle may feel very foreign for quite some time. After all, they have no connection to the one who is gone. They have no sense, no appreciation, of our life with that person, our life "before." It is like being in a foreign country where no one knows of our life back home, except that in this situation "back home" cannot be found anymore, for it has gone with the one who is gone. Although it lives within our hearts, it is invisible to those who did not know the landscape of our old lives.

When we have lost someone dear to us, most of us slowly get to know people better who were only acquaintances before. Slowly, too, we begin to meet new people for the first time since our loved one has gone. And yet it seems inconceivable that we could form any significant relationship with them. We refuse to believe that life will go on in meaningful ways with anyone else.

Others of us may jump into relationships, leaving no space to feel our loss. This is another way to deny death.

> One man I knew went to sleep each night touching the pillow on his wife's side of the bed. In the morning, when he awoke, he straightened her side of the bed. He lived in a protracted grief in which he seemed to recognize that she was gone and at the same time denied that she was. He wanted to move to a new apartment and begin again, but he could not let himself meet new friends or invite anyone to his home, lest the past be disturbed, like some wrinkle on his wife's pillow.

This man's situation is extreme, and yet it expresses the struggle that we all have in letting new beginnings enter our lives.

As new friendships and courtships begin to form, we are gradually amazed that our hearts can open and love again. We do love again, and yet it is a different love. We are surprised at how many different kinds of love we are capable of. We find that no love takes the place of any other, and we come to know the uniqueness of each person, of each love. We are surprised that our aliveness comes back —and to its full depth. We laugh again, we are excited again, we make plans again, we go on. Sometimes, in the midst of all this, we become quiet, we feel an ache in our chest, and tears well up in our eyes. We are confused for just a moment. Where am I? Who are these people I am laughing with? What is this foreign country I have made my new home in? And then we go on, assured that we are not betraying our past: we are not leaving our loved one behind, we are not forgetting. No, we are carrying our loved one's essence in our laughter. We are bringing the best of our love, and their love, to enrich our new relationships.

During this week, look around you. Look at the people in your life. At work, at school, in your social circle. Are there people you could imagine getting to know better, perhaps becoming friends with? Are there people near you whom you have already begun to be close to? Can you make some connection to one of those people this week? If you can, say to yourself, I will let the new into my life. I will open the door of my heart and come out and say hello. I will go on.

Knowing grief,
I can help others
in their time of loss.

I sit quietly and ask myself, What helped when it seemed that nothing would help? In the vast sea of mourning, where everything seems dead still and tumultuous by turns, there are memories of comfort. Because I was numb, I could not fully register these comforts. I could only sense them as one senses a touch to a part of the body that is anesthetized. And so it surprises me that the touch of comfort remains so vividly indelible in my memory.

Notes I received from people I barely knew who reached out to touch me with their memory of my daughter. A single white rose brought quietly in a vase. I still have that vase, and it still holds a consoling quietness. The friend who phoned every morning throughout the summer, not to talk, just to say, "I love you." The friend who knew one of my favorite spots near the water. He invited me to sit there with him on Easter Sunday, but I could not yet even get dressed to leave the house. He said, "Come on, you look fine in your bathrobe," and we drove to the pier and sat there talking quietly for a long time, not minding the strollers in their Easter bonnets. My cousin who came in and out of my home—somehow knowing when to come and when to go. A colleague calling to let me know that I was needed on a project—just to let me know I was needed somewhere as soon as I was ready.

There is much more I don't recall, because pain has a way of wiping out memory. And yet it surprises me that I recall so many of the details of the solace given to me. So many reachings-out. All so simple. Nothing extraordinary. Simply human. Just touching. Touching so that I know I am not lost, not forgotten. Human light beckoning on a sea of grief, like a lighthouse signaling the way back to a ship lost at sea.

In this way we learn the way of solace, by recalling the solace we have received, knowing that there is nothing we need do or say that is out of the ordinary, that it is exactly the simple human gesture that is most healing and most remembered. Anything that comes from within that feels real will reach the heart of the mourner, will touch her numbness, and tell her that she is not alone.

I can think of no greater solace during grief than to feel that you are not grieving alone, that you are thought of, loved. The comfort of others weaves a circle of love around the mourner. It is a healing circle. Each gesture of solace adds to the circle. No gesture can be too small, for it is by the gathering of all the small gestures that the circle is made. It holds the torn heart of the griever in a circle of tenderness and helps the heart to mend.

It is in being given to that we learn how to give. Because we have been given comfort in our grief, we are able to comfort others in their time of loss. And so it is that comfort ripples from one heart to another, binding us with compassion, moving onward even toward those in the world who mourn and whom we do not know personally.

As I write this, I am sitting in the park. There is a woman opposite. I look at her. She is a woman like me. There are smile lines on her face. And there are lines of loss to be seen there. She is like me, and like you, made of tears and smiles. We smile toward each other, a comforting smile, a ripple of knowing between strangers. And in that moment we belong to the human family.

During this week, use your journal to write about what has given you comfort in your grief. As you begin to write, let the words come, let the feelings come. Let yourself come to the heart of what has touched you so in this comfort. In this knowing, you will also be inscribing for the future what comfort you will give to others.

The spirit
of my loved one
is alive.

Our physical senses are not strong enough to hold on to the voice, the facial expressions, the touch of a loved one who has gone. Our sense impressions die when those who made them are no longer here, and their disappearance feels like a terrible loss for us. We want to hold on as long as we can to the smile, the way the head tilted, the walk, the sound of the voice of our loved one. But this all washes away in time, like a castle made of sand.

I will always miss the way my daughter looked up at me when she awakened from her nap, the way my friend Nina looked out at the world with Christmas-light eyes, the way my father laughed. These are so faint in my heart now. I strain to hear, I strain to see, but it is all faint, like the sound of a bird in the far distance. Something else, though, remains, and instead of growing weaker inside, it grows stronger and strengthens us. This is the essence of those we love who have died. We make a home in our heart for those we love. They planted the seeds of themselves in the soil of our hearts. Our love goes on and on, and the essence of the other grows as a part of our love.

As time wore on, Sally found herself saying "hi" as she passed someone she knew on the street or made eye contact with a friendly stranger. This "hi" was full-hearted, a greeting that had a warm smile. It was the hello of a full-bodied person. It was a new way for Sally to say hello. It was her husband's hello that she used to admire so much. Her own way of saying hello had been reserved, shy. The hello of Sally's husband had become a part of her. It helped to transform her shyness. She carried her husband's special quality as a new part of herself.

The ways, the qualities, the values, the essence of the spirit of one who has left goes on in us. Yes, there is a darkness, a light that has gone out with the physical going of a loved one. But the meadow always remains green, watered from the underground stream where the other lives within us. The essence of the other flowers forth in our living.

During this week, meditate on what it is that you want to carry on of your loved one who is gone. What is already a part of you? What is the essence of this person that is dear to you? Write of this in your journal. As you do, you are nurturing the seeds of that which will go on with you as part of your life.

Sometimes grief feels as though it will go on forever.

Isaac is out in a restaurant with his wife. An older man and a younger man walk in together and are seated at the next table. There seems to be a special closeness between them. They are apparently grandfather and grandson out to dinner together. Isaac looks at them for a long time. An old grief, an old longing and love for his own grandfather washes over him. Isaac goes on eating, keeps on talking with his wife. When the two men get up to leave, he says good-bye to them as if he knows them well.

I am at the supermarket, rushing to get my shopping done. Company is coming for dinner. I'm in a good mood, humming as I go up and down the aisles. As I turn down an aisle, I see a mother ahead of me, holding the hand of a blond little girl. I stop humming. From the back, she looks just like my little girl who died twenty years ago. I walk slowly behind them. I let the sudden sorrow wash over me.

It takes a moment. Then I walk beside them, untangling them from my past. I look at them and smile as I see how lovely they are together. How precious they are.

There are echoes of our love all around us. When they are heard, the door of grief opens, whether it has been two months, two years, or twenty years after someone has died. Someone recently sent me a picture postcard of a series of doors. Looking through one door, you see another, and another through that, and so on, until way in the distance, through all the doors, you see a pinpoint of a door. Beyond that you cannot see, but you wonder if there is another door. These are the doors of grief, seen at a greater and greater distance, but still there.

As we stand at the first door of grief, little things, unexpected things, will open a deep wound, a welling up of tears. The first snow. Passing an old couple on the street who are blessed to grow old together. At the beginning doors of grief, moments such as these will open a gaping hole.

As time passes, the first snow, a couple walking arm in arm, an elderly couple sitting on the bus and holding hands will tap on a distant door and call up love. A wistful love. A tender love. Tears may come, but they will not be the tears of heartbreak. Rather, they will be tears of "I know that, I have been there, that is precious." Tears and smiles will blend as the doors become more distant.

I do not think it matters that we go on with our lives, form new marriages, have other children. There is a way that the wound of grief still opens. I once told a friend of mine that there is a wound in us that has healed but will never entirely close. She said, "Then it cannot be healed. Once a wound is closed, it cannot open again." I recall being stunned by what she said. It sounded so logical, so reasonable that it should have felt true. But I do not think it is true. The wounds of grief do close. Like the doors in the photo, they grow more and more distant. But they are always there to open because grief is entwined with love, and love can never be destroyed, never disappear.

During this week, see yourself standing at the doors of grief. See which door you are standing at. Look at the door and see what is written on it. See the door just beyond and know that as you move to stand at this door, you come to a door that offers you solace. Stand there, see what solace is here for your grief now. Is it listening to a piece of music? Taking a walk alone or with a friend? Each day this week, stand at the door of grief and then move to the next door, the door that tells you what you need in this day for solace, for healing. And then look into the distance. Look through it, past all the doors, and find there the door of your love. The door of our love is the ultimate door, past all grief and past all sorrow.

I live open
to the unknown.

□

I am sitting and writing at a desk in a house in Taos, New Mexico. The house sits out on the mesa, a vast, flat stretch of land. There are few houses around. I am here alone, sitting at the desk, looking out the wall of window, out at the vast sky, filled with shifting clouds moving in the bright blue sky. Maybe it will rain. Maybe it won't. The only sound I hear is that of a bird. I can see it fluttering its wings out the window. The sounds of the thunder are distant across the sky. Will it rain or won't it? Questions. The answers unknown. It will rain, but when? I don't know.

Life is lived on the edge of death, and the terrain of that edge is always unknown. Always, our life is wrapped in the unknown. Most of us live our lives as if we know, as if there is no insecurity woven right into the heart of our existence. We go about busy with our plans, secure that they will happen. But truly, we do not know.

Facing the reality of a loved one's death helps us to realize that we do not know, that we live in a constant state of unknowing. And when death comes, we are shocked, and our secure sense of knowing what is in front of us is shattered. We realize that our former knowing was an illusion that veiled the insecurity of living without knowing, without being able to control life.

When my daughter turned four years old, she would wake me in the morning with, "You know, Mommy, I'm going very far away." "Where are you going, Leslie?" I would ask. "I'm going where it never rains, where it never snows, Mommy. And you can't come with me. It's farther than the sun and farther than the moon. It never rains there. And it never snows there, Mommy. And you can't come with me."

At that time, I thought my daughter was playing a game out of her very active imagination, and we went through the same litany every morning for several weeks. Soon after that Leslie became ill very suddenly and died ten days later.

What my daughter was saying to me was unknown. That she would become ill suddenly and die before her mother and father was unknown. Why she refused to wear anything but yellow in those weeks before she died was unknown. A little yellow butterfly sat on the railing in front of me on the terrace outside Leslie's hospital room. When it flew away, I returned to Leslie's bed, and she was just leaving the cocoon of her body. The story of yellow is unknown.

We live with these unknowns and unknowables. They leave a great open space like the open sky in front of me as I write. They bring open space and mystery and insecurity into our lives. They erase a smugness that we may have had, of "I know this," for at the bottom we know how profoundly we do not know. These unknowns open up love for what is fleeting, for what comes out of and returns into mystery. We reach our hand out toward what approaches us out of the unknown, stays with us for an unknown time, and returns to the unknown from where it came.

During this week, be aware of the unknowns and unknowables that are woven into your life. Even as you look at the faces of those you have known for a long time, family and friends, let yourself sense how there is something of them that is a mystery to you. As much as you think you know them, be open to something in the core of them that you can never know. Be aware of how much more a mystery they are to you than you ordinarily allow yourself to sense.

I learn
to live with
acceptance.

I heard a story once of a man who every morning placed a folded piece of paper in each of his two pockets. The paper in one pocket had written on it, "I am made of dust and I will return to dust." The other one said, "Today the world was created just for me." Carrying in both his pockets, and in his awareness, these two realities, he went about his days.

If I imagine knowing this man, I see someone living with an awareness of his death, not denying it, knowing that he is made of clay. At the same time, I see him living according to an old Hasidic tale in which it is told that when the world was created, man was not able to hold God's creation, and so it shattered, dispersing an infinite number of sparks of creation out into the universe. It is said that these sparks are hidden in everything we touch: people, tools, trees, animals, stones. Every time we are with the things of our world, with loving kindness, with gratitude, we are raising these sparks up and joining God in the ongoing creation of the universe.

Thus, each morning, this man, many men, many women, hold creation in their hearts. They do their best, they give their best, knowing how short their stay on this earth is. They take their dust and they take their darkness and they raise it up to the light. They raise up their own light, which has been in the exile of grief. And this is how I imagine this man who holds in his pockets the messages of our dual reality.

When we live with these realities, there grows in us an acceptance of how our frailty, our darkness, dwells side by side with our loving. Acceptance does not mean a bitter resignation to a fate we cannot change. In acceptance, we turn toward things that are greater than ourselves, accepting the great silence that underlies all of life. We accept that we are infinite, part of the great silence—and that we are dust. Both messages are carried in our pockets.

As we learn to live with and accept our loss, each thing we have becomes whole unto itself. A meal, a walk with someone, a friendship, a sunset—each thing suffices unto itself, is filled with life, is a wonder. And then later we forget again, the veil falls, we take life for granted, we take air for granted, we take our loved ones for granted. We cannot help but forget, for we have many concerns and our hearts go dull. But once having been shaken alive by death, we remember, too—we remember again to wake up, to touch the papers in our pockets.

See for yourself this week. Take two pieces of paper. Write on them, "I am made of dust and I will return to dust," and, "Today the world was created just for me." Carry these papers in your pockets. Touch them now and then during the day. Meditate on them, on their meaning for your life. Touch them when you are looking at someone, talking with someone, eating a fruit, drinking a glass of water, looking at a flower.

Life becomes simpler for me.

Life becomes simpler for me as it becomes more precious. I do not need to crowd my time and space with people and things and activities. I wish, rather, to have less doing in my life and more of a sense of being. Life spreads out before me like a whole cloth. Whatever I have is a whole. It is very simple. Eating a grapefruit is a whole. Nothing is fragmented anymore. My life has become simple and whole.

This is what Leo wrote in his journal at some point in his journey through grief. His life did change in a very visible way. Before his wife's death, he had been very busy with business appointments and family obligations. He and his wife seldom ate dinner at home or spent relaxed weekends together. They led very complicated, stressful lives. After his wife's death, Leo was hit hard by grief and could not continue the pace he had been used to all his adult life. He was stopped by sorrow, and in the course of the months that lay ahead of him he discovered himself in ways he had never known before.

Leo discovered the simplicity of setting his table and eating a simple meal that he had prepared for himself. He would light a candle, sit quietly for a moment before eating. He would eat slowly, tasting the food as if for the first time in his life, noticing the colors. He began to invite friends to a quiet Friday evening dinner rather than going to a restaurant. He began to value the quiet company of his friends, the sharing of a simple evening, simple walks, realizing that these experiences carry in their simplicity all the depth and beauty of life.

It was not hard for Leo to come to this simplicity. It began in his grief. As he sat doing nothing, spending hours by himself, he would notice the curtain in his living room moving in the breeze. He noticed the way in which the leaves of the plant were touched by the light. He noticed things that he had never noticed before, simple things that touched his heart and seemed to say to him, "This is life." Simply, he was there, simply the plant was there with him. Leo learned to love the ways in which simplicity touched him. His heart learned to choose simplicity, because whenever he did he felt powerful, he felt that he had given himself the space and time to be touched by the preciousness of life.

During this week, take the time each day to be simple, to do something simply. Begin with a fruit. An orange, a grapefruit, an apple. It doesn't matter. Sit and hold it. See its color. Feel its texture. Smell it. Picture where and how it grew, from a seed until the time it ripened and came to your hand. Peel it slowly. Be with the simplicity of just peeling a fruit and realize the miracle of this simplicity, this fruit we eat all the time. As you eat it, really taste it, eat slowly. Savor the wholeness that you can know in simplicity.

The human family
becomes
my family.

Death helps to teach us that we are all one. We are not separate from anything, from anyone. We all live, we all love, we all have a heart that yearns, that hurts, and we all die. We all belong to one another. Isn't it strange that death can teach us this?

Debra showed me a photo from a magazine. It was of an Ethiopian mother holding her child during the drought there. The child's stomach was swollen, its eyes wide with hunger and fear, staring into the blank, drawn face of its helpless mother. Debra cried. She sat quietly, holding the picture, no words, only her tears. After a while she said, "I feel like that mother, too. I am crying the tears she is too stricken to cry. She is going to bury her baby soon. I want to stand beside her. I want to be there for her when her baby dies. I want to share my water with her. If she is without water, I cannot fully have mine."

The veil of separateness dissolves when we go through grief. The stream of our connectedness flows beyond the limits of our own home, family, race, country. Something has happened in the depths of our heart. Its boundaries are dissolved. We know now that life and death are one circle, that the whole human family is one family. Our heart hurts when we hear of others hurting.

A stranger who saved a boy who had fallen through the ice while he was skating was asked why he had risked his life for someone he didn't even know. The man said, "I couldn't have gone on living if I had stood there while that boy died and hadn't tried to help him." This man, in that critical moment, broke through into the reality that we are all one. He knew in that critical moment the essence of life, that his life and that boy's life were one.

This knowledge of the oneness of all being brings to us a sense of compassion—the ability to touch a heart, to ease a pain, to lift someone up. We cannot always live in this compassion, but once knowing it, we have it as a light to hold to, to return to, to be guided by.

During this week, hold this light of your compassion. Place it in your heart and carry it with you. You may even see the color of this light. Wear something that is the color of the compassion you see in your heart. This will help you to remember. Carry your compassion to where it is easy, to your loved ones, to those familiar to you, who are like you.

And then send it out from your heart to those you do not know, those whom you have always thought of as different, as separate. Take them into the circle of your heart, know their humanity as your own. In this way you will be peaceful within yourself, and you will send peace out to this world that so needs it.

The planet
becomes
my concern.

A Vietnamese monk by the name of Tich Nat Han, who saw many of his people killed, has said that the trees are our lungs and the sun our heart. Without the trees, we could not breathe, even if we still had our lungs. Without the sun, we could not live, even if we had our heart. Everything on this planet belongs to everything else. It is as if we were all one body: the heavens, the oceans, the fish, the forests, the animals, we humans. If one part of this one body dies, it affects every other part. The fabric of this incredible universe was woven with all the strands made to hold one another together with love and care.

Grief teaches us of the preciousness, of the sacredness, of all of life, of all these strands. A drop of water seen with the heart is as precious as a pearl. In the eyes of a cow stricken by a drought, we hear the question, "What have you done?" We ask ourselves this question. What have we done to our waters, to our ozone layer, to our rain forests, to our whales, to our earth and sky? We feel the pain, for we are the intelligence and the heart of this living body that is our planet.

Once opened by the knowledge of death, of loss, of grief, we cannot easily get lost in our separateness. We can try, if it hurts too much, to keep our hearts closed, but somehow when the veil of separateness drops, it is really not possible to turn our back, for the heart pulls us forward with its open feeling.

Isaac shared his experience of visiting the Taos Indian Pueblo in New Mexico:

I was walking around the Pueblo, the home where these Indians have lived for 900 years. There was a group of about a dozen of us being led by a young Indian woman. We came to a stream of water. She pointed up to the mountain from which the stream came. She said, "That is a sacred mountain. No one can take photos of it. Even the Indians are allowed up it only for religious ceremonies. The water that comes from that mountain is just about the only pure water that flows in this whole state. We don't put anything in it." I asked her if it was okay to drink it. She said yes. I went down to the stream, cupped my hands, and lifted this pure sparkling water to my mouth. I drank it, washed my face with it, put it to my eyelids. Without the least expectation, I burst out crying. The beauty of this water, the purity of it. I loved it. I felt this terrible ache of sadness for what we had done to our waters. I was embarrassed for all the tourists standing there, seeing a grown man crying. But the Indian guide came over and touched me. She was crying too.

Isaac's tears were for both the utter beauty and purity of the waters of life and for the death of our waters. Tears for the beauty—and for the suffering.

Let yourself now follow your heart. Close your eyes, focus your attention on your breathing. As you breathe quietly, relaxed, see yourself in a spaceship floating outside the planet. Look at our planet and see it as it was just when it was created. See its freshness, its aliveness, the way it was in its original nature.

Now take a deep breath and see the planet the way it is now. See what has become of it, what we, the intelligence of the planet, have done to it. Now take another breath and know deeply in your heart what it is that you can do to heal the planet. See deep into your original nature that lives in your heart. See what you are doing as you return to the planet and know that this will be your part in making the planet whole again.

I live
in the awareness
of my own death.

□

You go to visit someone who is dying in the hospital or at home. You sit, hold a hand, and hear something inside that says, "It's him, it's not me." We go to a funeral service and we hear the same inner voice, we sense the curtain between them, the dead, and ourselves. But this curtain is only a thin veil. Behind it there is a deeper awareness within us that knows that we, too, are dying, that every moment we are dying, that we never know when we shall be dead. In our deepest knowing, we live in this state of being aware of our death.

When someone close to us dies, we meet death on intimate terms. The veils of our illusions drop and we cross the boundaries that separate us from death. We touch death, smell it, taste it. Meeting death in this way dissolves our misconception that there is any separation between life and death. We begin to glean that death and birth, living and dying are a circle, ever turning, without beginning, without end.

The religious traditions have ways to help us learn to

live within the knowledge of this circle. In one of the American Indian tribes, at a certain age, tribal members dig their own graves and spend a week in them. They are initiated to live with death as a part of their lives. In the Jewish tradition, when a man marries, he receives a white coat. It is the coat that he will be buried in. Thus the cycle of life and death is built into the ritual and helps us to remember. Without such ritual, it is easy to forget, and in forgetting, we lose something vital for our lives. Confronting the death of a loved one is like a ritual for us, to help us remember by letting fall the curtain of illusion that separates us from death.

In living with death as a part of life, we live differently. Don Juan, a Mexican Indian, told his student, Carlos Castaneda, to live with death always on his left shoulder, to live in the reality that death is always sitting there.

Imagine living this week with the awareness of death sitting on your left shoulder. The petty things we concern ourselves with, the time we waste doing what we don't want to do, the putting off until next week, next month, next year the things we long to do, the concerns we have of what others will think or say about us, the letters unwritten, the kiss or touch not given, the way we pass another human being on the street, knowing that they, too, carry death on their left shoulder.

Even if it is only once each day, bring your awareness to your left shoulder. Bring your awareness to how this knowledge changes the moment for you. At some point, at the beginning of the day, either before getting out of bed or in a time and space that you have reserved for being alone, close your eyes. Be aware of death on your left shoulder and ask yourself, What does my heart want in this precious day? What does it need in order to unfold my life in this day? Let your heart tell you. Follow it.

I try
to understand
all of this.

It is August now. I am sitting at a table high up in the mountains at a writing retreat. It is a place I have come to be by myself, to be quiet, to hear what is inside of me that wants to be said as I finish writing this book, which has felt like writing a long letter to you. But also I have been writing to myself—for whatever I have tried to convey to you, I, too, need to receive.

As I write, my heart tries to understand, to penetrate the mystery of: I am dust, my skin will decay, my bones will shrink and perhaps break as I age, I will become frail and I will die, and that will be the end of that. At the same time, my experiences with death, sitting with my daughter, with my friend, with my father, with my dog, after they died, sitting with them for a long time has let me know that they were not only their body. What I saw in front of me lying on the bed was an empty shell out of which a spirit flew like a butterfly, free, to the light, forever light. The mystery that we are dust to dust, that I am flesh, has me live with an ache always for those I have lost. At the same time, they are all around me, shining in the light.

And so I sit and I ask myself: Who am I? Who are you? Where are the people loved by us who have died? Sometimes I feel painfully cut off from them. But there is some deeper knowing part of me that awakens in quiet moments like these, in which I truly know that birth is not really a beginning and that death is not really an end. In these moments I know that death is the end only of a particular form, a particular body, although the loss of that form is always heartbreaking.

As I sit here I understand why I sense my daughter when I hear a bird sing or see a sunbeam. The light that she is, the clay that she was, nourishes all that continues to live and grow. She is part of the bird's song.

The same is true of the loved ones who are not here with you. They are a part of all that is, their light circulates in the body of light, their clay circulates in the body of earth. We die when we die. And too, nothing dies. We are born when we are born. And too, nothing can be born. Only our forms are forever changing. Only love is changing, forever changing its name.

I know that I will forget this knowing. And so will you. But the seed of understanding has been planted and will grow deep into our hearts. Plant this seed into your heart, this seed of "I am dust. I am light. I die. My form changes. I am always love." Plant this seed into your heart this week. Do not try to understand with your mind. You will not. Only with our hearts, and slowly, will true understanding take root.

Life goes on. . . .
Death goes on.

The wheel of time turns and turns. Just as I come to the end of these weekly Thoughts on grief, the wheel turns once again toward death in my life.

Today, my mother had a small stroke. First, she lost the use of her left arm. She dismissed it: "It's just arthritis. I'll go to bed and I'll be fine in the morning." In the morning, her arm was fine but her left leg felt dead and wouldn't move. Tonight, my mother is in the hospital, being observed, tested, and evaluated. And I wonder, What does that mean for an eighty-four-year-old woman? When her doctor said, "Perhaps we will need to do an arteriogram," I thought, An arteriogram on an eighty-four-year-old woman who tells me that she is no longer afraid to die? Why? Why do we keep trying to stop death as if it were our enemy? To the doctor I said, "I think you need to take that up with my mother. I do not believe that she would wish to have any invasive procedures performed at this point in her life." And then I thought, If my mother has such a test, maybe she can stay here longer . . . longer . . . longer. . . .

When I think of my mother dying, there is a part of me that is not so grown and adult a woman. A part of me is back at the beginning of grief. Numbed and squinting my eyes, raising my brow, as when we do not believe, cannot understand. No matter how many times I grieve, I always come back to the beginning of grief. It does not seem to become something I do better with practice, for each beloved needs to be mourned fully.

The other day, I heard a story of a young man who discovered his mother dead when he went to her room to see why she had not awakened at her usual time. He told his friend later that he did not feel sad for his mother's sudden death, because he knew that she was at peace. I have trouble with this kind of response to loss, which is usually thought of as highly spiritual. It seems to me to deny the human element—the pain that is felt by the mysterious human heart, no matter how spiritual our outlook.

When my mother dies, she will go. She may go in peace and be in peace. She is a beautiful spirit and I will feel the presence of her light. And I will miss her. And I will not know where she has gone, even as she seems to be all about. And I will always be her child and wonder like a child and ask the questions that a child asks. And never really know all the answers. Now, as my mother is beginning the last transition of her life, I feel like the three-year-old granddaughter of a friend of mine.

My friend Helen found a dead cricket in her house. It seemed very beautiful to her, so she left it on the table where she found it. As the sun streamed through the window, it lit up the colors of the cricket's skeleton like a rainbow.

When Helen's granddaughter came to visit, she saw the cricket there on the table and asked, "Why

can't it fly?" "It's dead," said Helen. That started Joy
on several months of incessant questions about death.
"What is death? Are you going to die? Am I going to
die? When are you going to die? When am I going to
die? Who's going to die first? What happens when
you die? Where do you go? And will I ever see you
again?"

One night, Joy woke her parents to say, "Let us
die together. I don't know how to die alone. I don't
know how to do it by myself."

Now, with my mother possibly dying, I feel like this
child. Yes, I speak with the doctors. I take care of all that
must be attended to. Yes, I feel other, more mature feelings
and think more mature thoughts. But as the wheel turns
again, I return to the beginning of grief, to the child within
me, to the questions that are no different from the ones Joy
asked of her grandmother. I want to ask my mother, "Do
you know how to do this? Can you do it alone?"

It does not matter that we must each die alone. The
question is still there: "My little mother, can you do it
alone? Because I cannot do it with you." I will be with her
as she does it. And I will go on asking the questions of this
great mystery that I am watching. These same questions
are asked by both the child and the philosopher, by the
young and the old. I think, But we who are older have
more to bring to these questions. Then I think, Perhaps and
perhaps not. I shrug my shoulders. I do not know if living
longer, knowing more, perhaps even having a touch of
wisdom brings more to our questions, to our quest to understand the unfathomable nature of death. Perhaps the
questions themselves are sufficient, all the questions that
little Joy and big Judith go on asking. Perhaps they are the

questions that express our awe toward life, our beholding of life, our love for it.

During this week, let the questions that are within you arise, and write them in your journal. They may tap some answers within you. These answers hold your philosophy of life. And in the places where there are only questions, the questions that arise within you are your beholding of life, your awe of it. Let yourself find your words for all of this. We do not always need answers. We cannot always have them. Sometimes the questions alone hold our full aliveness and participation in the mystery of life.

Where am I?

Some time ago, a teacher told me of a memory she carried from her childhood in Germany. She recalled that a traveling circus would come each summer to the small country village she lived in. All the children would gather in the meadows, having waited a year for the circus people to return. Always, the circus show began in the same way. The clown would come before the children, who were sitting there on the grass with their eyes opened wide with anticipation. And the clown would shout, "Are you here? Are you here?" And the children would shout back, "I am here! I am here!"

Whenever I call the clown to mind, I hear that voice shouting to me, "Where are you? Are you here?" Too often, I am not. My eyes well up with tears, for I know that I am hiding somewhere, hiding some part of myself, of my life, not fully alive. I want to shout back to that still small echo of a still small voice, concealed but present to the heart that wants to hear. I want to shout back, "I am here. I am not hiding." But too often I am not able to shout back. I cannot find my full voice, my full aliveness. At such times, there is a feeling of profound sadness, of loss, for not being all that I uniquely am, for not fully living the life that I could be living.

I have come to believe that each life has its own unique design. Just as each snowflake and each flower has. Perhaps I have come to this sense by knowing so keenly through loss how special each person lost has been to me. Through death, we discover how precious the design of each life is. Each life is unique and each life is a gift, including our own life. Each life answers, "I am here!" in its unique way.

How do I know my design, the deep expression of my lifetime? We know it by listening to and following our heart, by listening to the still small voice that calls to us from deep within to be who we are. Thus, we hear people say, "Follow your heart, follow your bliss, follow your truth." I call it living our life with intention, consciously creating our life, unfolding its design. In this way, we make our life all that it can be, as if it were a material in the hand of an artist, a creator. And truly it is. This precious material, this clay, this spirit, this design of our destiny that calls us to life is our blessing.

Living an intentional life means knowing that life can be created, to some extent, by us. What we do with our time, how we are with others, how we show our love and concern—all are our own decisions. And an intentional life is also a life of practice. In practicing who we want to be, we become who we really are. In this way, our life calls out, "I am here." Each Thought in this book is accompanied by an exercise that you can practice in your life. They do not necessarily need to be done in order. You can always go back to those that especially call out to you. They are there for you to return to.

And now, another exercise that can bring to you a practice with which to unfold yourself: Let yourself be comfortable, breathing easily, closing your eyes. See yourself looking for the part of yourself that is hiding. See where you are, see what part of yourself this is. Call out to yourself, "Where are you?" Follow until you come to yourself, the part of yourself that wants to be found, that wants to be. Lift this part of yourself up to the light, like a prayer. Hold yourself there in the light. See yourself whole, as you long to be, as you truly are and are capable of being. See yourself in your true design. See what you look like, where you are, what you are doing, how you are living this moment with the intention of your heart. See yourself going on in this way, unfolding yourself in this way in the world. See yourself living the gift that is your life.

Find yourself in this way, each day of this week. As you hold yourself up to the light, see yourself in the light of your true being. Each day, at least once a day, find a way to express your full self in your life, and as you do, be aware that this is living your life with intention. Sense how your actions, how your gestures toward others, are calling out, "I am here."

A prayer
for going on.

When I was a young student, I believed that everything I read on the printed page of a book was true and that every author was an expert. Now I finally know that that is not true. I am no expert guide on this journey of grief. I struggle to find meaning, to go on with intention, just as you do. I can only hope that I have shared the way of my own journey and that perhaps something I have said has touched you in some meaningful and comforting way.

And so, I do not have any last words of wisdom to say to you. When all is said and done, I can only be quiet and listen to that still small voice. I have never been quite sure of what prayer really is. When someone tells me that she has prayed, I always wonder what she has really been doing. But I am too embarrassed to ask, thinking everyone knows but me. Someone once said that prayer is to listen very deeply, to be quiet and to listen, until one hears. Perhaps, when all is said and done, the words we are left with are those best found out of listening deeply and letting the heart find the words and do the speaking. These words spoken by the heart are what I think of as the seeds of prayer that are spoken into the vast womb of the universe, holding our hope there and having it call us toward life.

Dear life, please hold my hope, hold my desire to give to life, to love and to serve life. And please hold my darkness, the tattered remnants of my grief. Place a star over my head to guide me when I feel lost. Forgive me my emptiness. Help me to know how full I am with the fullness of my heart and with the essence that I carry of all those I have loved who are gone. Help me to remember always the unbreakable circle of love. And when it is my turn to die, please let me be mourned, for this will mean that I, too, was loved and that I lived in some way that could be missed.

And now, listen to your heart's prayer. Sit quietly, close your eyes. Listen. For as long as it takes. Set this time aside to listen until you hear. Let your heart speak its desire, let it speak aloud. Hear the still small voice move through your spoken voice. Write down in your journal what is said. These words are your prayer. They are the seeds of your going onward, of renewing life. Take them and cast them into the universe, where they can be planted and grow and carry your intention, your heart's desire. May all the seeds of all our prayers be planted, may they grow, may they heal us and our planet into life.

ABOUT THE AUTHOR

Judith Sara Schmidt, Ph.D., is a transpersonal psychotherapist and teacher who lives and practices in New York City.

THE
THOUGHT
-A-WEEK
GUIDES

Each book contains 52 insights, one for each week of the year to help you achieve your goals effectively and efficiently. Designed to give you expert advice, each volume is written in an up-beat, informal style by a specialist in each particular field.

TA-162